WORDS AND MONEY

WORDS AND MONEY

ANDRÉ SCHIFFRIN

VERSO

London • New York

An earlier version of this book was published as
L'Argent et les mots by La Fabrique 2010
First published by Verso 2010
© André Schiffrin 2010
All rights reserved

1 3 5 7 9 10 8 6 4 2

Verso
UK: 6 Meard Street, London W1F 0EG
USA: 20 Jay Street, Suite 1010, Brooklyn, NY 11201
www.versobooks.com

Verso is the imprint of New Left Books

ISBN-13: 978-1-84467-680-4

British Library Cataloguing in Publication Data
A catalogue record for this book is available from the British Library

Library of Congress Cataloging-in-Publication Data
A catalog record for this book is available from the Library of Congress

Typeset by Hewer Text UK Ltd, Edinburgh
Printed in the USA by Maple Vail

Contents

Introduction

Ten years ago, in *The Business of Books*, I described the conglomerate takeover of publishing that has transformed the world of words. Where publishers had been satisfied with profits of 3 to 4 percent throughout the twentieth century, the new conglomerate owners wanted returns much closer to those they had gotten from their other media holdings—newspapers, TV networks, and so on. The pressure to earn at least 10 to 15 percent, if not more, profoundly altered the output of the major publishing houses. In the US, these new, often foreign conglomerate owners had come to control 80 percent of all trade books.[1]

The conglomerates are international. Nonetheless, reactions to my book in individual countries varied. Most American reviewers agreed with my analysis, but in Britain, with the surprising exception of the critic on the *Financial Times*, everyone denied that anything could possibly be wrong. At the time, many believed that the pattern

---

1   André Schiffrin, *The Business of Books*, London/New York: Verso, 2000.

of conglomerate takeover I described, and the subsequent demands for much higher profits, was a phenomenon limited to the English-speaking world. French and Spanish reviewers and others who discussed the book, which eventually appeared in some 25 countries, agreed that while the situation in the Anglo-Saxon countries was certainly dire, a similar one would never occur in Europe. Certainly not in France, homeland of *l'exception française*, where cultural diversity was built into the country's very system.

In recent years, I have been spending half of my time in Paris and have therefore been able to monitor closely the transformations in Europe. I have followed the enormous changes that have taken place following a similar shift of ownership from independent publishers to international conglomerates, many of them based in Europe. But I have also noted the countermeasures that European countries have used to try to control these changes. Some of these are based on policies that have been in place since the Second World War, and in a few cases from even before then. Others, particularly those aimed at the press and the Internet, have been formulated only in the past few years. And some are still evolving, such as the response to Google's attempt to digitize much of Europe's cultural heritage. Although Europe's political contexts—and basic assumptions—often differ greatly from those of the United States and Britain, the alternatives that are being explored in Europe are important, and many of them have not been reported on in the English-language press, and certainly have not been considered as possible models.

The purpose of this short book is not only to describe these but also to see what the European experience might mean for the United States and the United Kingdom not only in publishing but in other media as well. Accordingly, in addition to chapters on book publishing and bookselling, I look at what has been happening in journalism and the printed press and with film and the Internet. Since these areas are even more globalized than that of books, there is an increasing amount of overlap between countries, raising both legal and political issues.

Nowadays, when I meet people in Europe who have read *The Business of Books*, they chastise me for having been overly optimistic. Things now are far worse than I described them then, or indeed expected them to become. For I, too, thought that the French system, in particular, would be strong enough to withstand the pressures of conglomeration and globalization. France had two major corporate media groups but also a third segment of influential, independent print entities as a counterbalance. This third sector included major publishing houses such as Gallimard, Le Seuil, and Flammarion that had done much to define French culture in the postwar years. These, I thought, were strong enough to stand against the global behemoths.

But a few years ago, in a book published in Europe called *Le Controle de la Parole*,[2] I described the first phases of the breakdown of the old French system. Gradually it, too, had been taken over by the large international conglomerates.

Ironically, it was the determination of Vivendi, the water and sewage company turned media conglomerate, to play the globalization game that brought about that company's downfall. Like its major competitor, Hachette, Vivendi wanted to break away from the constraints of French publishing and follow the pattern of the Anglo-Saxon media giants. But its purchases of film studios and

---

2   Paris: La Fabrique, 2005.

publishing houses in the United States were extraordinarily inept. Though the head of Vivendi, Jean-Marie Messier, enjoyed his fame in the New York press—which praised his Fifth Avenue apartment and his donations to the Metropolitan Museum of Art—his newly created empire soon fell apart. His major publishing purchase, the venerable Boston publishing firm Houghton Mifflin, for which he paid 2.2 billion euros, had to be resold the following year at a loss of some 450,000,000 euros, an incredible sum that was barely reported in the press. Had Messier ordered his publishing houses to focus on producing only literary fiction and poetry for the rest of their existence, they would not have been able to lose even a fraction of that amount. By the time Messier was forced out in 2002, Vivendi had 18 billion euros of debt, presumably including the 25 million euro loan to himself that Messier wanted forgiven, in addition to his $12 million severance payment.

The firm that was responsible for close to a third of French publishing—its book group became known as Editis and included such famous names as Plon, Laffont, Nathan, Bordas, and Pocket—had to find a new owner. Happily, according to the French papers, a white knight was in the offing. Baron Ernest-Antoine Seillière, head of the vast investment firm Wendel and president of the French employers association, MEDEF, offered to buy Editis. This would keep French publishing in French hands, something the French press and government cared strongly about, even as its own publishers were expanding their holdings abroad. As one might well have expected from his roles, Seillière was known for his very conservative views on social and economic questions and not known for any particular interest in cultural issues. Furthermore, his was a curious decision, since firms like Wendel liked to state that they expected a return of 25 percent on their investments, beginning from their very first year. To the few who wondered whether professional investors were truly interested in the long-term development of French publishing, Seillière answered specifically that Wendel had no intention of immediately reselling the firm. They would keep it on for a minimum of 10 or even 15 years, an assurance that no one in the press or in the government questioned. One would have thought that those in charge of monitoring the acquisitions of major firms would have at least required some sort of written commitment. But presumably the baron's word sufficed for a government—Sarkozy's—whose own principles were so close to those of the MEDEF.

A mere four years later, Seillière announced that he was selling Editis to the Spanish publishing and television giant Planeta. He was doing so at a great profit for Wendel, which had bought Editis for 650 million euros and was now selling it for over a billion. But Wendel's real profit was far greater even than that. As is usual in such deals, it is the firm that has been purchased that assumes most of the debt in the transaction and is expected to pay it back, so Editis assumed some 425 million euros of the debt incurred by Seillière when he bought it. So Seillière's own real investment had only been 225 million euros, and his profit close to an incredible 300 percent, according to the calculations of the financial daily *Les Echos*.

In keeping with the methods of such buyouts, Seillière had obtained the cooperation of Editis's top management by offering them a share of the promised profits. The impressive sum of 37,000,000 euros was paid off to these executives, a generous example of profit sharing for the few. The head of Editis was allowed to invest 700,000 euros in the deal in 2004, walking away with a capital gain of 11,300,000 euros in 2008. The management of Editis, their loyalty having been thus purchased, proceeded to follow policies that would maximize profit until the firm could be resold. Seven additional publishers were bought, including the very commercial XO, and distribution fees were lowered to add as many new customers as possible. Management decided to enforce a draconian policy of cost controls, to make the firm as attractive as possible to future purchasers. No raises were given during the three years, departing employees were not replaced—everything was done to give Editis a very attractive 11.9 percent profit its last year. Faced with the news that the staff had been literally sold out, the company's union protested vehemently and was finally grudgingly granted a risible bonus of 1,500 euros per employee. The baron was so satisfied with his good work that he gave himself a special multimillion-euro reward, which so angered some members of the Wendel family that they began a series of stockholders' suits against him.

But Seillière had demonstrated something important: one could still make money from publishing. Not, of course, by selling worthwhile or even profitable books, but by buying and selling the firms themselves. He showed that he had learned his lessons well and had become the true face of modern French capitalism. Apart from an angry op-ed piece in *Le Monde* written by the head of the Editis employees' union, Martine Prosper (who has since written a very useful little book called *Edition: l'envers du décor*[3]), the press remained relatively silent. No one suggested taxing these remarkable gains—Seillière having already

---

3   Éditions Lignes, Paris, 2009.

been one of the Frenchmen to benefit from Sarkozy's huge tax cuts for the very rich, which were even greater than Margaret Thatcher's in Britain.

Forgotten too were Seillière's assurances of a long-term commitment as well as the horror of seeing a large chunk of French publishing sold to a foreign owner. That flag had been raised a few years before, in defense of Hachette's putative purchase of Editis, despite the prospect of two-thirds of French publishing being put in one hand. Now no one mentioned the old patriotic arguments.

Indeed, few in the press even bothered to look into Planeta's reputation in Spain or the plans that it might have for its new holdings. These, indeed, are still unknown at this writing. The one paper that did file a story from Madrid, *Les Echos*, discreetly mentioned a few items that might have caused concern. Planeta, it stated, is known for the secrecy with which it guards its figures: "It is not a champion of financial communication." Nor is its owner, José Manuel Lara, whose personal wealth is estimated at two billion euros, making his the sixteenth-largest fortune in Spain. In addition to investing in TV and in airlines, Lara owns several newspapers, including *La Razon*, the most reactionary of Spain's dailies, politely referred to by *Les Echos* simply as Spain's seventh-largest paper. Of Planeta's annual turnover of 2.5 billion euros, publishing has accounted for a little under 2 billion, making the group by far the most powerful in Spain. But along with Hachette, now the largest publisher in England as well as in France, these two firms are still at the bottom of the international league of publishing conglomerates. The biggest, the Anglo-Dutch firm of Reed Elsevier, does 5.7 billion euros of business a year, closely followed by the English firm Pearson (incorporating the *Financial Times* and Penguin) with 5.2 billion. Hachette is ninth on the list with 2.1 billion and Planeta last, with 1.8, less than a third of the biggest firm's takings.

Lara has doubtless discovered by now that the profits boasted of by Editis had come partly from the severe cost cutting and other measures described above. We will have to wait anxiously to see what Planeta intends to do with the group that includes some of France's best-known publishers as well as the country's one remaining major left-wing firm, La Découverte.

The Editis example is not only fascinating in itself; it shows the kind of profits that major investors are looking for. The biggest commercial publishing firms try to show that they can make more than 10 percent a year, but that's considered really slim pickings for the Wendels of this world, who have demonstrated that they can make 300 percent.

The current economic crisis revealed that the really big money wasn't coming from the mundane activity of making actual, tangible goods and then selling them. The banks and others had gambled with their investors' money, using it to create incredibly complicated financial products that could then be sold to unwitting purchasers. Seeing the tremendous profits gained by these dealers in abstract goods, traditional investors began to feel left out. We see this in the American newspaper industry, where for years an annual profit of 26 percent has been considered normal. When the Knight Ridder chain of distinguished provincial papers had the misfortune to make a mere 19.4 percent profit in 2005, its owners were quick to sell it off, which resulted in some of its best papers being closed down. The current crisis in the American press is largely due to the heady expectations of recent years rather than to a realistic consideration of what newspapers might normally earn, a subject to which we will return later in the chapter on the press.

Newspapers, of course, have not been the only medium to suffer in the current crisis. Book publishers have had to greatly reduce their production—and their staffs—during the current economic downturn. A diversified, independent publishing field, with many smaller firms, might well have survived more successfully. But the conglomerates, with their high profit expectations, have acted in the hope of preserving those profits rather than publishing the best possible books.

To be fair, the publishers are also suffering from the concentration of booksellers, a process that in many ways they aided and abetted. Now that the chains have destroyed most of the independent bookstores, they hold the fate of most books in their hands. In the US, the major chain Barnes & Noble has been losing money these past few years. Its chief rival, Borders, is reputed to be on the brink of bankruptcy and recently closed 150 of its mall stores—close to half of all its outlets. As a result, both chains are extremely reluctant to take on books that do not have an assured sale and indeed have returned as many of these unfortunate items as they could, raising the publishers' return rates to historic highs. Even before the economic crisis, the chains would buy a minimum number of intellectual titles, usually 300 for the 1,000 stores in the Barnes & Noble chain, most of which would be returned. Now even that figure has diminished, and the independent bookstores that could be counted on to stock these titles have nearly disappeared in the big cities. As I've pointed out, Manhattan, which in the postwar years had some 333 bookstores, now has barely 30, including the chains.

A parallel development had taken place in England, where the Waterstone's chain, which had driven many of the independents out of business by its use of deep discounts, was itself bought up by the WH Smith chain of newsagents. Long known for its commercialism and political caution, Smith soon changed its new purchase into a chain focusing on discounted paperbacks. The chances of a reader, in England or America, stumbling on a new book he might not have realized he wanted, are dim indeed. As is the future of most independent bookstores.

Surely no capitalist in his or her right mind would invest in a bookstore these days, or in a publishing house, or in a newspaper. The profit in owning a bookstore is negligible, if not nonexistent. The large publishers are having great difficulty reaching their target profit of 10 percent. And as we shall see below, the newspapers, too, are no longer delivering the huge profits that investors had come to expect of them.

What is the future, then, of these and other institutions in a world whose investors consider them insufficiently profitable? Can we continue to rely on the traditional forms of profit-centered ownership? We are in a transitional stage—more and more people seem to recognize this, but almost no one has offered a vision for the next stage, or a way to get there. And yet, in the realm of culture—music, theater, dance, even cinema—most countries have long accepted that public support is essential and not-for-profit structures necessary. Now we are faced with a group of other media—book publishing and its distribution infrastructure, newspapers and other newsgathering organizations—whose profits are no longer high enough to satisfy the private sector but for which no other sources of support yet exist.

Are there alternative possibilities? What can we learn from efforts that have already been made in different countries to establish new models? While many of the solutions described in this book may seem utopian to American and English readers, they are mostly policies that have been in place for years and have proven that they can work. The newer policies, especially in the field of newsprint journalism, have yet to be tested. But they all spring from a willingness to develop new models rather than assume that many of the traditional media, such as newspapers and printed books, are doomed. The traditional market, I argue, has not shown us how to preserve the kind of diverse and independent culture that we know we need. The question to decide is how we may maintain much that we still believe is necessary in our modern democracies.

1

The Future of Publishing

One of the reasons the development of publishing throughout the world is so interesting is that it is truly a microcosm of the different societies in which it exists and a mirror of the way in which modern capitalism has evolved. Technically, there is no inherent reason for publishing to be very different from what it was in the nineteenth century. Until quite recently, it still followed the traditional artisanal model rather than the modern corporate one, and in fact was not so different from the enterprises Balzac describes in *Lost Illusions*. More important, publishing was seen as a profession, not just as a business. People who were really interested in making money did not choose it as a career. Though of course publishers needed to make enough to keep their companies going, none expected the business to be wildly profitable. As I pointed out in *The Business of Books*, the average profit of publishing houses throughout Western Europe and the United States, during much of the nineteenth and most of the twentieth century, was in the range of 3 to 4 percent per annum, roughly the amount of interest paid by a savings bank. Until the firms began to be bought up by large media conglomerates, only a few decades ago, that percentage was considered perfectly adequate. It was only when the new owners began to compare the profits of their publishing houses with those of their radio networks, television stations, newspapers, and magazines that they began to worry. How could they justify "subsidizing" their book publishers at the expense of their other holdings? This is the way they often explained their position. Surely the publishers could manage to earn at the very least 10 percent a year, if not 15 percent, bringing themselves into line with what the others were making.

As I have argued, this entailed not only a major change in what was being published but in the attitudes of those running the publishing houses. Coming up with these new figures became the primary goal, to be accomplished within a fiscal year—or even better, on a quarterly basis. Growth was another "target," as it is euphemistically called, and the largest conglomerate, Bertelsmann, publicly called for 10 percent annual growth as well as 15 percent profit, a policy that forced publishers to continually seek out new companies to buy, since there was no way that such growth could be produced by the books already being published.

Gradually, publishers became investors, bankers of a kind, desperate to find both the best sellers and the new firms, or acquisitions, that would satisfy their new owners or the banks that had lent them the money they needed. Accordingly, the heads of the houses felt that their pay should be closer to the salaries of bankers than to those of the editors they once had been. Not, of course, the billions paid to the gamblers and traders of the last decades. But at least something in the seven-figure range. When I first started in publishing in the 1960s, the highest salary in Britain was a notorious 10,000 pounds a year, which of course was worth much more then than it is now, but still infinitely less than today's wages. But most publishing salaries were similar to those paid in universities. A senior editor might make as much as a professor, a beginner the equivalent of a lecturer. By the time I left Pantheon, then a part of Random House, in 1990, its president was making well over a million dollars a year. Others were making even more, the highest at the time being $2.2 million, for the head of McGraw-Hill.

Within the houses, editors are now judged by the amount of money their books made. Careful tallies are kept, and the young editors I interviewed in recent years knew to the last decimal point what their annual profit was. I remember once interviewing a young editor who wanted to leave Oxford University Press. What were our signing quotas, she asked me. I wasn't familiar with the term, so she explained it meant that she had to sign up books that would sell at least a million dollars' worth of income for the firm, and that at a famous university press!

While visiting China earlier this year I was astonished to see the degree to which they had developed a similar system. I had not been to China for more than twenty years and was curious to see how publishing had evolved there. Certainly the bookstores showed a great variety of books being published, particularly books explaining the workings of a capitalist economy. In Shanghai and Beijing, the major bookstores had whole walls filled with texts on business management. I went to visit an old colleague, who had been an intern at Pantheon Books in the late 1980s, just before my and my colleague's departure. He now headed one of the major Beijing publishing houses, doing over $100 million of business every year. I asked him and his colleagues how they were remunerated. Their basic salaries were generous by Chinese standards and, while not as high as in the West, were certainly better than those of their academic counterparts. But the basic salaries were supplemented by a percentage of the sales of any book that might become a best seller, and these bonuses could easily double an editor's income. When I asked how their books were chosen, my old colleague laughed embarrassedly and said, "That's easy. It's whatever will sell best." The system was geared to ensure these results, and everyone was "incentivized" to ensure maximum profitability. The lessons of the business management texts had been well learned, and once again, publishing showed itself a microcosm of the greater society, marching with the rest of China toward a new and very thorough form of capitalism.

What is striking is that changes of this nature have been taking place not only throughout the world but also in what used to be known as the liberal professions, careers that used to be primarily free of the pressure to make money. A few years ago, I gave a talk to a reunion of my Yale University classmates, all graduated in 1957. When I described to them the change that had taken place in publishing, many came up to me to complain that the same had happened in their fields. Lawyers were rewarded according to the amount of money that their clients brought, and "rain-making," finding lucrative clients, was the most important activity. Architects told me they were no longer expected to build the most beautiful buildings they could design but simply to maximize the amount of rentable space in the containers they were expected to fashion. Even doctors explained that they could no longer practice medicine as they wished but were expected to deliver whatever care was most profitable to the hospitals in which they worked, skimping on those patients with the least insurance, using the most expensive machinery on those who could best reimburse the ever rising costs of medical care (including spiraling administrative costs, since multimillion-dollar salaries are common among the heads of hospitals).

None of these changes were due to the internal demands of these professions. Indeed, they are contrary to the needs of the practitioners and their clients. But they were part of the inevitable monetization of modern capitalist society, which allowed for no exceptions and was ravenous in its demands. What we have seen in the last couple of years has been the temporary collapse of some of the most extreme parts of this exercise. The banks and investment houses were unable to control their greed and increasingly gambled with the money that had been entrusted to them, while expecting to be rewarded with vast amounts as a result. Even though their system collapsed, many of its proponents have continued to defend it and have returned to their former practices and their obscene remuneration.

The system has proved remarkably able to defy the consequences of its failures. In the United States and Europe, bankers and speculators have stubbornly defended their outrageous salaries and bonuses. In the City of London, bankers were arguing that England would lose its role as a financial center if financial salaries were curtailed, and bankers in other countries made similar arguments. Aided by the same governmental officials who urged the deregulation of the markets in all of these countries, the financial sector has been able to stave off many of the reforms that at first had seemed an inevitable consequence of the crisis and the public anger that accompanied it. In the United States, President Obama surrounded himself with the very officials who had been in large part responsible for the crisis. We have yet to see what, if any, reforms can be imposed by the left-of-center governments of Britain and the United States, and "any" becomes less likely with every passing day.

The question that those interested in books and the media must ask is whether this new form of capitalism will prove to be interested in an area that has, at best, limited profit potential. As was stated in the introduction to this book, the best a publishing house is able to produce in the way of annual returns is well below what the banks and speculators hope for from a business and have come to expect. By applying the methods of leveraged buyouts to publishing, it has been possible for a handful of businessmen to make millions, but at the cost of abandoning the interests of their firms and of their colleagues. The economic crisis does not appear to have changed the way these investors think. The 25 percent per year that groups like Wendel expected to make from their publishing venture was not based on the housing boom or even on the gambling of traders. It was what seemed to them a reasonable return on their investment. As we have seen, this can be greatly exceeded by buying and selling publishing houses, but not by simply producing and selling books, even the most commercially successful.

It is too early to predict exactly what will happen to the large publishing groups. But we have already seen the pattern to expect, even before the economic crisis that greatly accelerated it. The pressure is to produce fewer books, concentrating on those with the highest sales potential, eliminating vast areas that used to be the hallmark of many of these houses. In the past I have joked that publishers progressed from infanticide, neglecting the new books that show no sales promise, to abortion, canceling existing contracts of books no longer thought to be financially worthwhile. The goal now is contraception, preventing such titles from ever entering the process at all.

In *The Business of Books*, I analyzed the contents of

five decades worth of catalogues from the largest houses. Some, like the output of HarperCollins, taken over by Rupert Murdoch in 1987, had changed so much as to be unrecognizable. Their lists from the fifties and sixties resemble what is now published by only the best of the American university presses. The current contents justify the firm's boast of being part of the "entertainment industry," tying in as many books as possible to the content of films and television. Even so, those managers who directed the transformation of Random House and HarperCollins have been let go, not having brought in profits enough to please their owners, whether Bertelsmann or Murdoch.

As a result of this concentration, fewer and fewer authors are able to find a publisher at all. Most of those who do find that they will not earn much from their books. Many calculate that they barely earn the minimum wage, considering the time it takes to write a book. In France, according to the union leader Martine Prosper, only 900 authors can claim an income of more than 16,500 euros a year from all of their titles.[1]

The pressure now is not so much to increase as to preserve profit. As always, part of the solution is to fire as many people as possible, and hundreds have lost their jobs in the large American firms during the current recession. They are unlikely to be hired back. Florence Noiville, one of *Le Monde*'s literary editors, has just published a fascinating book called *J'ai fait HEC et je m'en excuse (I Went to Business School and I'm Sorry)*[2] in which she shows how the major thrust of the curriculum at France's leading business

---

1 Martine Prosper, *Édition, l'envers du décor*, Paris: Éditions Lignes, 2009.
2 Paris: Stock, 2009.

school is not to show how business or the economy works, but to teach its students how to maximize profit, partly by firing as many people as possible. These graduates have found willing employers in most conglomerates, and one can see their training at work. Likewise, in America as in Europe, there is a growing trend toward centralization, with the conglomerates amalgamating what used to be independent firms into larger entities and thereby eliminating even more jobs. We now see in the literary pages of the *New York Times* the curious ads of what is called the Knopf Group, in which books that once were published by houses as diverse as Doubleday or Pantheon—which used to be at opposite ends of the publishing spectrum—are now listed without mention of the putative publisher, "publisher" having clearly become an unimportant and even meaningless label. The remaining staffs have been merged under one centralized management. Reports from France suggest that the same process may have been started by Planeta as it begins to examine the overpriced Editis group it now controls.

None of this is to suggest that the large conglomerates will fade away, as some have suggested. They will doubtless continue, publishing best sellers and benefiting from the sales of their backlists, built in better times. Their new output will continue shrinking, as they limit production to provide the required profit. This will be a difficult time for the many good people still working for these houses, trying to protect what they have been able to do in the past and fighting to the best of their ability the unending pressures from their owners. But even they will admit that more and more of the books that they used to publish, and would still like to publish, are coming from the small independent houses that have begun to spread in recent years, both in Europe and in the United States. (In Italy, literally hundreds of new houses have been started in the past decade.) The flourishing of these small independent houses is an encouraging sign, particularly since young people have started many of them. But they face enormous difficulties, both in distribution and in covering their costs. It is calculated that the major distributors demand a minimal sale of 300,000 euros a year to take on a publisher. This excludes most of the smaller firms, which have to work out their own system of distribution and sales fulfillment. While the smaller houses account for a third of the 38,000 titles published annually in France, their total sales come to less than 1 percent of the annual volume.[3] In the US, the small publishers account for a similar tiny percentage, though the number of intellectually important books is far greater. Until recently, the hundred or so American university presses also accounted for less than 2 percent of total sales.

I was struck on a recent visit to Rome by the enormous difference between the books offered in a large bookstore chain, like those of Mondadori, and the titles displayed in one of the few independent stores. Those seeking the latest best sellers would have no difficulty finding them in the large chains, at a discount, but would find practically none of the smaller, more demanding titles. Those were all in the independent stores. A similar difference can be seen in New York. When a large Barnes & Noble store was deliberately opened next to one of the few remaining independents, the St. Mark's Bookshop, the owners of the latter were understandably worried. When they looked closely at their new competitor, however, they found

3 Prosper, *Édition, l'envers du décor.*

that only 4 percent of their own stock was on offer at the larger store.

In Europe as well as in America, small publishers have the same difficulties in breaking through to the chains. I was told, proudly, by Feltrinelli that Italy's now one-hundred–store book chain would offer to display your book in all its shop windows, for the modest fee of 10,000 euros, clearly a prohibitive price for a small publisher. The French chains, like their Italian counterpart, charge high fees for prominent display of a book, near a cash register or in a prominent floor bin.

Increasingly, small houses publish the difficult translations, the demanding books of nonfiction, the new and untried authors. Some, like Amsterdam in Paris, have even ventured into magazine publishing, launching a French equivalent of the *London Review of Books*, *La Revue Internationale des Livres et des Idées*, which has managed to break even within a year, selling some 8,000 copies. But of course its contributors are not paid and its staff live off minimal salaries. One of the most successful French firms, intellectually, Agone in Marseille, pays all of its staff minimum wage, including its director. The publisher of the French edition of this book, Eric Hazan, has yet to pay himself anything in his firm's first decade and is unlikely ever to do so.

So the independents run on courage and self-sacrifice, explained in part by the youth of so many of their most active editors. But this is hardly a safe structure for the future, and some means must be devised to protect this effort and allow it to expand. In France, some governmental help has been available, on a limited scale. Several regions, particularly those in the Île-de-France and the Rhône-Alpes, have developed intelligent and courageous programs, at a time when the national government has been intent on reducing the budgets of its cultural ministry. This effort is largely centered on helping specific books and series and has made available important books that would never have otherwise been published. Île-de-France, unable to offer blanket support to small publishers, has focused on aiding specific projects. For instance, a start-up grant of 40,000 euros was given to the tiny new publisher Les Prairies Ordinaires, to allow them to translate a series of demanding works by authors such as the feminist theorist Judith Butler and the American historian Nelson Lichtenstein. Thanks to their publisher's minuscule overhead, these books can break even at 1,500 copies. But the grant has now been exhausted, and the future of such translations is far from guaranteed. A similar grant was given to the publishing house Amsterdam to publish in French the most important English and American research on the Atlantic slave trade, one of the most exciting areas in recent historical research. A grant was also given to La Fabrique to reissue new editions of nineteenth-century French historical classics. Agone received substantial help to translate, for the first time, major works by Karl Kraus and Alfred Döblin. (Similar help is available in Geneva for francophone publishers, and in North America Quebec in particular and Canada as a whole have very impressive programs allowing their publishers to keep pace with their massive competitors in the US and in France.)

These countries' regional authorities, similar to the United States' local councils for the arts and humanities, have much bigger budgets than their American counterparts. The Île-de-France authorities mentioned above, who are notable for their daring, have an overall annual budget of 55 million euros, 4.3 million of which is devoted to books.

This is close to half of the entire budget of the American National Endowment for the Arts, $161 million.

Aquitaine, a far smaller region, still has a cultural budget of 21 million euros, 2 million of which goes to books. These regional budgets mean that some 237 small provincial publishers outside the Paris region still got 4 million euros in aid in 2005 to help produce and market 275 titles. No comparable support exists in the US, though in the United Kingdom, the Scottish arts council has been very generous with local publishers.

The CNL, the Centre National du Livre, is France's major source of help for publishers, bookstores, and libraries as well as for aid with difficult titles and translations. It is a model for what could be done in the US, the UK, or other countries that wanted to give substantial help to authors, publishers, and booksellers. Its budget, 37 million euros for 2008, dwarfs that of the regional entities and encompasses many major national efforts. Its 300-page annual report lists thousands of grants, some very large. Ten million euros this year has been devoted to the digitization of the books in France's National Library, a major challenge to Google's efforts to establish a monopoly in this field.

A large part of the budget is devoted to areas that ordinarily might be in the domain of the foreign ministry. Major amounts are granted to translate French books into foreign languages, coming to more than a million euros, in line with the traditional French policy of spreading French culture throughout the world. Even more money, 1,615,000 euros, is allocated to translating 330 foreign books into French. That makes an interesting contrast with America's National Endowment for the Arts, the closest thing to a ministry of culture in the US, which in 2009 allocated $200,000 for thirteen translations.

In addition to this, the CNL has ambitious programs across the book world. It spends 500,000 euros a year helping libraries buy new books (overall, the French government has helped to double the number of public libraries in recent years). The translation grants are part of an overall budget of close to 6,500,000 euros spent helping publishers in various ways, one million of that devoted to subsidizing scientific and scholarly publications. It has also spent 375,000 euros supporting the publication of poetry and drama, and close to 2 million paying for France's many literary festivals. [4] These involve some major projects, such as Les Belles Etrangères, which brings authors from different countries on tour throughout the whole of France and has an impressive following. Bookstores are also helped in many ways, which I shall describe in the chapter devoted to them.

Overall, this is an impressive effort and could be the base for additional, more daring funding. There have been some criticisms of the CNL, which is run by classic French civil servants. Decisions are made by independent commissions, representing the profession and the universities, which has the advantage of creating a democratic framework but the disadvantage of mirroring the current intellectual consensus in the universities. Thus these decisions tend to be predictable, with 80 percent of all money disbursed going to the large firms and to much more conventional projects than the regional ones mentioned above. Moreover, in keeping with French bureaucratic tradition, decisions are not explained and no list of rejected projects is available. Some of the younger

---

4   These statistics, from 2008, are available on the CNL Web site at www.centrenationaldulivre.fr.

independent publishers have complained of this lack of transparency.

Nevertheless, all of this money has obviously been very helpful, even if on an ad hoc basis. But no publisher can count on the CNL and regional disbursements to plan its future. What other ways must be explored to offer these fragile structures some kind of permanence? What examples can we draw from what has been tried to date? It would be encouraging to say that the traditional family-owned independent firm is still an obvious choice. But such firms have become increasingly rare and will become rarer, as death duties force the sale of firms after the first generation. Few are the investors willing to take on what is bound to be a marginal enterprise. Therefore, some of the alternative solutions must be structural. Even though many, if not all, of the small publishers I've mentioned are de facto not for profit, there are some advantages to establishing a de jure not-for-profit status, as we did when starting the New Press in 1990. In all countries, such structures are free from taxes on their profits, a usually irrelevant benefit, since usually there are none. But they can also receive tax-free donations from individuals, foundations, and governments. This is what allowed us to get the New Press off the ground, and American law is particularly open to such entities. Forming a cooperative is another possible alternative. Unfortunately, efforts to start writers' coops, in Germany and elsewhere, have been hampered by disagreement among the coops' members. In Sweden, a readers' coop, Ordfront, has worked well (with 20 thousand subscribers, only 10 percent of the membership need buy a title for the book to succeed), though it has not yet been emulated elsewhere. But coops made up of the workers within the firm, all with a common goal, are a logical possibility. I suspect

that most people in publishing would be happy to work in a book equivalent of the 1960s experimental watch-making coop Lipp. That now legendary coop succeeded in taking over a failing company and having its employees run th firm. They did so brilliantly until the government decide to pull the plug by canceling its orders. Though France no boasts some 2,000 coops, employing over 50,000 peopl new coops have not yet been started in the many failin firms. This is partly because, for some reason, the gover ment has refused to grant the same initial help to coops th it does to other start-ups. But there is no reason why tl might not be changed under a more progressive leadersh

In the United States, foundations have been a ma source of support, but they are still relatively rare Europe. (An interesting exception is the Kurt W Stiftung in Germany, which was recently establis to help that country's growing number of indepenc publishers.) It is probably easier to get outside hel the publisher can be associated with a university or o established cultural entity, though as in all such cases, 1 editorial independence has to be guaranteed. For what reasons, there has been little progress in this area, but t are very successful precedents to point to. In *The Bus of Books*, I mentioned two outstanding examples. One in the unlikely locale of the University of Southern Illi which gave office space to a new literary publisher c the Dalkey Archive, which specializes in translatior the reprinting of major foreign literary works that a longer available. The university also paid one of its l ture professors part of his salary to direct the firm, was independent of any of the university presses Dalkey Archive has become one of the major sour translated literature in the US, its editor coming to E

to look for titles just as the editors of such major American literary firms as Knopf and Farrar, Straus and Giroux used to do. Dalkey's example has inspired a number of others, so that the University of Rochester, for instance, now houses a similar effort called Open Letters.

As I have mentioned elsewhere, when the New Press began, it was offered free housing, in an admittedly very dilapidated building of the City University of New York, which helped us save the hundreds of thousands of dollars which would have had to be spent on rent. The same university also gave space to the not-for-profit Feminist Press, which has been one of the few institutions of the women's liberation movement to survive the movement's recent decline.

Another example is the highly successful Raisons d'Agir, started by Pierre Bourdieu from his office in the College de France, which quickly became one of France's most effective publishers of political texts, some selling in the hundreds of thousands in a field that at the time had been largely abandoned by the major publishers. Yet in spite of these encouraging signs, no other universities have followed suit. Yet nearly all major centers of learning include a university press, some of whose offices and facilities could easily be lent to a small and independent parallel effort. Such an initiative could come both from local would-be publishers and from the faculties of the universities themselves. In the United States there are over one hundred university presses, and though these have increasingly tried to become regional publishers of guides, local history, and the like, they have not tried to expand in a more important way. In France and Italy, many of the university presses are still in the business of publishing the more recondite works of their faculties. It does not seem unreasonable to ask the universities to look into

their potential intellectual and cultural role, particularly in a period where, as we have seen, both the media and the large publishers are cutting down severely on their intellectual output.

It is not only universities that can help in this effort. I recently visited the offices of Cheyne, one of France's leading publishers of poetry. Such an enterprise would not be expected to generate much profit, and its founders were only able to start it with the help of the village of Chambon-sur-Lignon, which gave the firm an abandoned schoolhouse. This is now a beautiful workshop and office, and houses the old printing presses on which many of its books are produced. After thirty difficult years, Cheyne has paid off all its debts and can feel assured that 65 percent of its sales now come from its backlist, a rare achievement in publishing. Clearly such an effort would not have been possible without an enormous amount of work, but the village's help was an essential component and demonstrates the support that even the smallest of governments can give. On a larger scale, the city of Minneapolis decided some years ago to encourage both intellectual and artisanal development. It devoted several buildings in its central district to welcoming publishers and craftspeople. As a result, Minneapolis is now the unlikely center of an impressive number of independent publishers, such as Greywolf, that have done much to embellish that city's progressive reputation. Minnesota seems to have been especially hospitable to not-for-profits of all kinds—and its leading city offers a much less expensive environment than does New York or San Francisco. Minnesota's council on not-for-profits boasts some 2,500 members.

I have stressed regional and local aid because in these difficult economic times not much can be expected from

hard-strapped and often conservative national governments. Though the CNL in France, as has been shown, is
still able to give considerable help, publishers themselves
are often wary of the political constraints that could come
with that support, particularly in countries such as France
and Italy, whose presidents are obsessed with controlling
the media. An obvious solution for France would be to use
some CNL funding in conjunction with regional support to
help smaller publishers pay their employees some kind of
minimum wage, in addition to helping them publish difficult books. Much of the CNL money comes from the fees
that are gathered from the photocopying of copyrighted
books. Part of this income could easily be designated to
permanently help these publishers. One or two million
euros a year, less than 5 percent of the CNL budget, would
go a long way toward assuring that these small firms could
continue to do work that everyone now agrees is vital.
Criteria would have to be established as to the quality and
predictability of the work, but these exist for other parts of
the book chain. As we have seen, the regions have chosen
their projects very well, but regional governments can
change and grants expire with no promise of continuity.
Given the amount spent annually by the CNL and similar
bodies in other countries, helping cover some of the salaries of the most imaginative and fruitful independent firms
should be possible without breaking anyone's budget.

Another, supplementary, approach can be seen in the
Norwegian example that I will describe in the next chapter. Buying a given number of books a year to distribute to
libraries throughout the country, as Norway's government
does, is an obvious way to increase access to important new
work while at the same time help publishers indirectly. The
purchase of 1,000–1,500 copies per title, sufficient for a small

country like Norway, could obviously not be expanded to quantities geared to the population of larger countries. But even that small number would make an important difference. Indeed, this is the number of copies that British and American libraries used to purchase before their budgets were slashed in the Thatcher/Reagan years. The total cost of the Norwegian program, some 11 million euros, is close to the help given each year by the French government to the cinemas of *art et essaie*, as I discuss in the chapter on the cinema below. I would suggest that we consider the idea of offering all libraries a supplementary budget to take on books that they might not be able to afford at this time. Libraries are now under the same pressure as bookstores to concentrate on best sellers, to buy those books that will be the most borrowed. It would be unrealistic to ignore such pressures, and libraries clearly have a responsibility to make such books available. But a supplementary budget for books the libraries would like to own but can no longer afford could solve the problem. Ideally, this would be for books from the smaller independent publishers, since there is no need to use public funds to subsidize the profits of the major conglomerates. Politically, this problem could be resolved by making the funds available for books published in small initial quantities, such as less than 3,000, the number usually considered to be the minimum that large houses can publish profitably, but well above the printings of many of the small houses (an average printing for the commercial houses in France is 8,200, though there are many titles with much lower first runs). There is no question here of the government's providing libraries with a list of books they must consider.

In making such suggestions, one might also look at the methods used to encourage French film production. There the state gives to certain approved projects an advance on future box-office receipts. Publishers could be given a credit toward the amount that they would eventually realize from library purchases, giving them the always necessary cash in hand that would allow them to publish that year's program. This would have the advantage of being a loan without being recognized as such. As we shall see in the chapter on bookstores, there is much to be learned from the way in which European film industries have been helped by the state. All of these ideas are relatively small, but practical and easy to implement within the European context. British and American government programs are nowhere near the stage that has been reached by their European counterparts, though in the past their support of libraries and universities was as great, if not greater, than Europe's.

In the US, foundations have usually been seen as the most important source of help where government failed to act. But for the most part, these institutions have not been willing to enter fields they consider primarily commercial. They see publishing and bookselling as Darwinian, ruled by the law of survival of the fittest, which in many cases means the largest. But the European examples given in this chapter could, in time, be implemented in the English-speaking world. Canada has already shown a willingness to protect domestic as well as French-language publishing and has spent a great deal of money protecting local publishing against competition from the behemoth to the south.

Realistically speaking, the situation in the US and the UK could best be improved by enforcing anti-monopoly laws already on the books. To stop or slow the increasingly rapid disappearance of independent bookstores and publishers, the most important step these governments could possibly take would be to use these laws to break up the vast media conglomerates.

But eventually it should be possible for them to follow some of the European programs detailed in this chapter as well. For that they will need both time and a growing public awareness of the costs of the media monopolies that now exist.

2

The Norwegian Example

It may seem odd to turn to Norway to find another way of thinking about the media. After all, the country is relatively small—4,650,000 inhabitants—and relatively isolated.[1] It has chosen to remain on the margins of Europe, refusing to join the European Union and keeping its own currency. It has a long history of cultural independence and from the beginning of the twentieth century has sought both to maintain local control and to encourage its own creative culture. In the immediate postwar period, the Social Democratic government received an open letter from Norway's artists and intellectuals arguing that the general public deserved greater access to culture, particularly in the underpopulated parts of the country. The government responded by setting up a traveling theater, cinema and art galleries. Over the years, it has built on these beginnings and gradually evolved a unique and now comprehensive cultural policy. Happily, it can certainly afford those luxuries. Thanks to North Sea oil, Norway is one of the world's richest countries and has the highest capital reserves, per

---

1   The figures on the Norwegian press and publishing industries in this chapter are the latest to come from Norway's official government sources.

capita, of any country, though it does not use these to pay for its current budget.

As early as the 1950s, Norwegian publishers felt that their books might be endangered. Most Norwegians can read Danish, and books from their larger neighbor were readily available, threatening their own, smaller publishing efforts. Fewer Norwegian books appeared, and they sold fewer copies. And Norway was not immune to the competing interests of the new consumer society that was spreading throughout postwar Europe—the new mass media, popular fiction from abroad, etc. By the sixties, however, the Norwegians had begun to establish the framework of a new and daring cultural policy.

I first went to Norway in that decade. One of the country's literary magazines, *Vinduet* (*Windows*), had asked me to write a Letter from New York, and I'd begun to know *Vinduet*'s editors and other publishers. Finally I decided I should visit the country and try to spend my accumulated fees, hoping to find a Munch print that I could afford. (I failed in this effort, though later others told me I could have succeeded had I been a little more diligent.) Norway was then still a very provincial and relatively isolated country. There was one newsstand in midtown Oslo where one might buy a foreign paper. (Returning to Copenhagen very much felt like rejoining the Continent.) My hosts proudly showed me the center of town with the Parliament on one side, the National Theatre on the other, and the café where all the intellectuals met in between them. But the bookstores were well stocked, as were the kiosks selling Norway's own papers and magazines.

I visited again in the early nineties, when my first book, *The Business of Books,* was published, and things had greatly changed. The North Sea oil had made the city far more prosperous and bustling. Back in the 1960s most locals had dined out at six p.m. and then gone home; now Oslo's town center was crowded with revelers until the early hours. One could have been in Spain.

The media landscape had also become much livelier. On arriving, I counted some 14 newspapers, and each had a page of book reviews. That particular day, they were all focused on recent Norwegian poetry. The papers ranged from the usual pink sheet devoted to finance to *Klassenkampen* (*Class Struggle*), which had, understandably, a somewhat smaller circulation. Altogether, the country puts out some 224 newspapers, 82 of which appear four or more times a week. A decade ago the largest, *Verdens Gang*, had a circulation of 370,000. But circulation has suffered in Norway as well as in the rest of Europe, and that number is now down by a third, to 284,000. But this is still close to the circulation of *Le Monde*, in a country with a population one-thirteenth the size of France's. Oslo boasts four other papers with circulations ranging from 123,000 to 247,000, according to the latest available figures. Each copy of the largest paper is read by an average of four people, close to a quarter of the adult population. The circulation of the dailies totals 607 copies per 1,000 inhabitants, the highest percentage in the world. Sweden comes next with 472 and Britain, which is usually thought of as a newspaper-soaked land, is third with 321.

Norway's newspapers do not thrive at the expense of other media, which also have high readership there. The Norwegian equivalent of *People* has a circulation equal to that of the largest newspaper. *Motor*, the largest monthly, claims more than 900,000 readers. In addition to this, Norwegians spend an average of 161 minutes a day listening to the radio, considered a moderate amount of time compared to other countries, and 150 minutes a day watching television. This seems to leave very little time for non–media related activity, and one must assume that people do several of these things simultaneously. By contrast, there is little watching of DVDs, and very few Norwegians seem to have a home computer—one in eight.

Norwegians have long agreed that a diverse press is an essential part of a democracy. As a result, there is some governmental help for minority papers. No money is given to any paper that pays dividends. But papers with smaller circulations, from 2,000 to 6,000, can be helped, and so can papers that are number two within a given area. There is also support for national papers considered major opinion makers in politics and economics, as well as papers linked to specific political parties. These subsidies amount to between two and three percent of the press's annual turnover. More important is the exemption of newspapers from the VAT, a privilege worth more than a billion Norwegian kroner ($170 million) annually. Everyone agrees that these subsidies should involve a total hands-off policy regarding editorial content.

All this diversity has not, however, meant freedom from conglomerate control. The three largest media firms control over half the national circulation as well as being involved in radio and TV. The best-known of these firms, Schibsted, has become famous throughout Europe for its aggressive development of free papers well outside of Scandinavia. It also owns substantial shares of various Norwegian provincial papers and 49 percent of the second-largest Swedish paper, *Aftonbladet*, as well as developing press ownership in the Baltic States. So Norway is not free from the patterns of capitalist press control that we see throughout the West.

The pattern of television control also resembles that of neighboring countries. There is a BBC-like national network, NRK, funded by an annual license fee paid by 1,670,000 households, resulting in close to 300 million kroner ($51 million). It and all local radio and TV stations with an "idealistic or ideological basis," to quote the government report, are exempted from all taxes. But there are also three other national TV chains, owned by the major Norwegian conglomerates and by their Swedish equivalents.

Books and publishing

Because of this heavy corporate investment in the mass media, maintaining an independent publishing industry has been a major government aim in recent decades. As early as 1965, an Arts Council was created on the British model to give support to all of the arts, throughout this physically vast but, especially in its northern parts, very underpopulated country. The basic aim was to guarantee publishers a minimum sale on certain volumes, which would be given to the country's public libraries, assuring readers broad access. Each year the Council buys 1,000 copies of 220 titles in fiction (including poetry and drama) for adult readers and 1,550 copies of 130 titles for young people. In a small country, this covers much of the worthwhile work published in Norwegian each year, and 100 translated novels have now been added to the mix. In 2009 a further 1,000 copies of 70 nonfiction titles were made a permanent part of the program. Fourteen cultural magazines are also given to libraries in the same way, while others receive grants for their production costs.

This is a great help to the publishers, whose normal print runs might often be below these figures, allowing them to continue to publish in fields they might well have abandoned otherwise. Authors, too, are assisted, since they get better royalties from these purchases (20–22.5 percent) than they would otherwise. The total cost for this ambitious program in 2009 was a substantial 11.3 million euros.

While the system largely depends on the publishers submitting appropriate books for the program, the Arts Council does have committees that read every book included. The council feels that overall the program is very successful and has been of enormous benefit to the smaller libraries scattered throughout the country. It has also helped deal with the anomalous Norwegian situation of having no fewer than three official languages, one a minority variant of the basic language, which is why there are two different national theaters in Oslo, and a third in the north, in the Sami language, spoken by the indigenous population there.

Given the size of the Norwegian population as a whole, the book program is a very ambitious and effective one, which has kept both publishers and authors alive in a globalized-media world that might have otherwise done them in. But even the absolute numbers are impressive when compared to those of other countries. The library purchases come close to the numbers that used to exist in the US and the United Kingdom, where publishers could once count on local libraries buying 1,000–1,500 copies each of new, worthwhile books. These budgets have been slashed, along with other public programs, beginning in the Thatcher/Reagan years. They have not recovered since then, in either country, eliminating a program that equaled the Norwegian one at least numerically, though practically providing these much larger countries with far fewer new library books per capita.

The Cinema

I have kept for last the most radical and also the oldest of Norway's programs, public ownership of the cinemas. When I first heard of this, I assumed it was a relatively recent response to the growing Hollywood control of distribution. Far from that being the case, the system dates back to 1913, and reflects several strong Norwegian national traits.[2] The early 1900s saw a flourishing of civic activity—libraries, workers' education groups, and local colleges were all part of the policies of both the Labor and Liberal parties. Municipal control of local cinemas seemed a logical extension of a potentially powerful educational medium. In addition to this, there was a national debate that had begun in 1910 on the possible harm that films might do to young minds, an issue that had already led Sweden and Britain to establish film censorship. So a mixture of classic Protestant morality along with Norway's strong interest in mass education led to a policy that gradually developed the public role in local cinemas. The process was opposed both by Norwegian film distributors and by Hollywood itself: *Motion Picture World*, then the leading American trade paper, ran a story headlined "Socialization of the Cinemas" that warned against "supporting the Norwegian Bolsheviks whose plans threaten the whole trade."

But attempts to boycott the Norwegians failed, and by 1932 half the country's cinemas were municipally owned, and these accounted for 90 percent of the market, a share that still obtains today. The cinema was seen as a cultural

---

2   The information on the evolution of the film industry comes from an excellent article by Nils Klevjer Aas that appeared in *The International Film Guide*, 1988, and was reprinted by the National Association of Municipal Cinemas in Oslo.

service, aimed at meeting local needs, rather than as a money-making enterprise. For a while, the cinemas also jointly tried to encourage a national film industry, concentrating on adapting literary classics to the screen. By 1936, these Norwegian films garnered a 10 percent share of the market. In the 1950s, the government extended these plans and eventually established a small ticket tax to finance them. More recently, in 1987, a Film and Video Act required all those showing or selling films and videos to acquire licenses from the local authorities, thus establishing local censorship as well.

The municipal cinemas together have formed a national organization that focuses on keeping local managers informed about the latest movies. They also run a traveling circuit to the remoter areas without permanent cinemas. Some 200 screens reach 130,000 viewers annually in this way, an extension of their public service mission rather than a money-making venture.

To anyone visiting Oslo, the local movie houses look like any others. There are the latest Hollywood blockbusters, but the managers can choose other films that won't be as profitable. Multiscreen cinemas that eliminate any movie that isn't immediately highly profitable are not part of the local culture. Independent and not-for-profit control has been maintained in this crucial area. Though Norway does not boast of the Norwegian Exception, the way France has vaunted its own over the years, the Norwegians have created a structure that in all areas of the media allows them to have that very thing. Unlike the French, they have not sold to outsiders the key institutions that make for cultural independence.

To be sure, having money in the state's coffers has helped make many of these programs, such as the book purchases, possible. But others, such as the local control of cinemas, were an early political decision. What is most impressive is that all of these programs together create a coherent cultural policy, one that has been carefully thought out over the years. In this respect, Norway's example is worth far more attention than it has received, and is worth emulating.

3

Films and Movie Houses

The situation of the movie industry shares many characteristics with those of book publishing and newspapers, but throughout Europe it has received far greater support from governments. It has been seen as a more important international expression of a national culture, and at the same time it reaches a broad, though diminishing, domestic audience. It is closely linked to television and what is shown on the smaller screen. And it also has the great benefit of substantial government aid programs that were established quite early in its history.

France is perhaps the most interesting example of such a system and how it works. The story goes back to 1948, when Leon Blum, France's former prime minister, came to America to negotiate terms for foreign assistance with US Secretary of State James F. Byrnes. The Americans were very hard on Blum and insisted on certain clear concessions before they would agree to give him any help. One of them was that American films be given free access to French cinemas. Before the war, they had not been widely seen in France, but by the 1950s, they would reach 25 percent of the audience, and by the early 1980s that number would double and half of all tickets sold would be for American films. (Their share in 2008 was still a very high 45 percent. Nowadays, the French have become accustomed to this and begin to worry only when their own share of viewers falls to 30 percent.) The issue at the 1948 negotiations was largely an economic one, though others have since seen the agreement reached as a major tool for spreading American ideas to Europe and introducing the American Way of Life to a continent that was more accustomed to discovering America through its literature. Clearly Humphrey Bogart and Marilyn Monroe were more persuasive ambassadors than William Faulkner and Horace McCoy had been before the war.

Though Blum had very little choice but to agree—France was in desperate need of American aid—his concessions were strongly attacked by the Communists. Their leader, Maurice Thorez, made veiled anti-Semitic attacks on Blum's importing of the American values of money and capitalism.

It is difficult to tell how much this weighed in the decision to protect and subsidize French cinema, though French film producers were forceful in protesting the results of the Blum–Byrnes accord. It was agreed in 1948 that a 10 percent tax would be placed on all film tickets and that this money would then be used to help both French film producers and cinema owners.

This became the basis of the system still in place today, which now brings in some 230 million euros of revenue annually (most of this from film ticket sales, with a small addition from taxes paid on TV ads). Close to 50 percent of this money is returned to the film producers, based on a complex formula that pays the producers back a percentage of the tickets to their latest film, stopping at 5 million viewers and reducing the percentage for the more popular films. Over half of the revenue, 75 million euros, is spent on supporting the production of new films chosen on the basis of their hoped-for quality. (Thus, American film producers indirectly pay for half of the help given to their French competitors.)

A relatively small amount, 10 million euros, is spent to subsidize the national network of art cinemas, the famous *art et essaie* movie houses that any visitor to Paris's Latin Quarter will remember. But the network goes well beyond these familiar houses, showing classic American films and mounting endless Bergman and Woody Allen festivals. Altogether, 1,045 of the 2,075 cinemas in France qualify as *a et e*. Multiplexes are now common in France, and we should note that the total number of screens is far greater, some 5,400, most of them controlled by the five largest chains: Gaumont, MK2, UGC, Pathe, and CGR, who together control 55 percent of ticket sales.

The figures are therefore very close to those in book publishing, where the two largest groups, Hachette and now Planeta, control close to two-thirds of all books published. The chains have argued that some of their screens qualify as *a et e*, largely because they show new foreign films that have only a limited public. But I assume that it is primarily for political reasons that the government goes along with this and grants them some of the aid allocated to the *a et e* cinemas. The amounts are based on what is programmed but also on the size of the audience, the amount of support the cinemas get locally, what ancillary educational programs are planned, and so on. A special effort is made to reach smaller towns, partially in the hope that the aid will diversify what is available, allowing their cinemas to show more foreign and classic films, gradually broadening the taste of their audiences.

Some of the local programs I have seen are very impressive, with a mix of new and popular films alongside a selection of classic and foreign films that is closer to what one would expect from a *cinemathèque* than from a small-town movie house. Many offer discussions after the film, particularly those films with political or social implications. Thus, the *a et e* cinemas play the role of social and cultural centers, in the way that many independent bookstores try to do. (In part because of these programs, some regional governments, such as Poitou-Charentes', have begun to help these cinemas as well as independent bookstores.) Similar public discussions, with film directors, academics, and others, became common in Paris when the program started in the 1950s, but are now less common in the capital than they are in the provinces.

Government aid to a given cinema can range from 1,500 to 50,000 euros a year, depending on what is shown and how often. This is a substantial amount and nationally is far greater than the regional help given to a few bookstores, which will be discussed in a later chapter. The smaller cinemas depend on this help not only to continue to show varied films but also to withstand the unfair competition that they get from the chains. In recent years, the chains have instituted substantial discounts, allowing viewers unlimited access for a fixed monthly sum. In addition to legitimate competitive tools like this, the large corporations use a variety of indirect ways to get more money from film distributors. They charge the distributors to advertise coming attractions in the cinemas and insist on the distributors buying ad space in the free programs they give to customers. All this is very similar to the way in which the publishing conglomerates will bribe the *grands surfaces*—France's supermarkets, which account for 20 percent of the country's book sales—to give their publishers preferential display space. And just as the publishers make sure that their own stores, such as Hachette's Relay chain of newsstands, are well supplied with books that look as if they will be best sellers, while independent bookstores are often left without copies, so the movie chains make sure that their own major cinemas get an adequate number of films (which can cost 800–1,000 euros per print to make, in this still predigital stage). In 2005, a group of independent producers protested the high number of copies of such popular films as the Harry Potter franchise and the Lord of the Rings series, which were filling more than a thousand screens on release, modestly asking that at least 10 percent of the country's screens be reserved for independent film. As we have seen in both France and the United States, the multiplex system can be deadly for less commercial efforts. If a film does not make the requisite profit in its first days, it can quickly be replaced by a more commercial title, even if that means that several screens are showing the same film. This is now common practice, and films are often not given the time to reach or create their potential audience by the old system of word of mouth. The same system is at work in the chain bookstores and the supermarkets. If a commercially promising book does not begin to sell in its first days, it is removed from its location at the front of the store to a less attractive location, before being returned to the publisher.

In addition to attracting important indirect income the French chains have been very aggressive in trying to block the expansion of the independents. When a chain closed one of its cinemas in the Paris suburb of Montreuil, it tried to keep an independent company from taking over the space. The chains have also fought to keep independents from offering tickets at prices lower than theirs (common in the smaller towns) and even, unsuccessfully, tried to get help on this from the anti-monopoly authorities. This behavior has led to the appointment of a special *mediateur*, an ombudsman who is called in to block the worst of the chains' actions, as when they try to keep the independents from getting copies of the latest, most popular films. There was talk of establishing a similar post for the book trade, but that effort seems to have died.

It can be argued that much of this is the normal behavior of conglomerates faced with competition. But part of the reason for this recent aggressive competitive behavior may be the chains' own fears about the decline of the film audience. Movies were very popular during the Second World War, when cinema offered the French one of the few possible forms of escape and diversion, and in the winter that rarity, a spot warm enough to spend a few hours. Though the films made then were determinedly apolitical, the war years produced some of the best of modern French cinema. After the war, audiences grew, peaking in 1957, when 420 million tickets were sold. Sales fell in the seventies and eighties, when the newly privatized TV channels took over much of the film audience, and 1992 saw a low of ll6 million, barely more than a quarter of the historic high.

Now there has been a rebound, to 191 million in 2008 (still less than half the 1957 number), though 20 million of these were for the incredibly successful comedy *Bienvenue chez les Ch'tis*. The movie ticket sales exist in spite of the fact that 5 million people now have access to more than 50 cable networks, many of which show nothing but films all day and night. DVDs, for some reason, have not proved to be as popular in France as in the English-speaking world, and are less of a threat than cable TV, though the price of subscribing to cable is high—close to 50 euros a month for full coverage.

Dramatic as cable and DVDs have been in their overall impact on the international film business, many more changes will be seen in the coming years. Digitization will mean that copies will be available for far less money, and the smaller cinemas will have greater access, though they will have to go to the expense of changing their projectors. European film producers will find themselves in a far more globalized industry, with American distributors beginning to invest in foreign-language films. At the same time, countries like India are investing in Hollywood firms like DreamWorks and offering millions to actors like Brad Pitt and George Clooney to make whatever films they want. These new ventures may well threaten the traditional dominance of the West in the world market, while strengthening the autonomy of countries like India, where only 5 percent of the films shown are American. The existing patterns of distribution will doubtless be disrupted or transformed.

For these reasons, the French system of protection and subsidy, both of film production and of independent cinemas, may become even more important. For all its faults and compromises, it has allowed a relatively diverse film culture to survive and, thanks to the *a et e* houses, continues to give French viewers a far wider choice than is available in the Anglo-Saxon countries.

The situation in the United States and the United Kingdom could not be more different. The spread of multiplexes in those countries has harmed the independent cinemas much more than it has in France. In his book *Rich*

Media, Poor Democracy,[1] the distinguished media critic
Robert McChesney notes that 10 percent of the films shown
in America used to be of foreign origin. Now that figure is
less than 1 percent. The multiplexes are quick to get rid
of any Hollywood film that does not sell as well as those
on its other screens. And multiplexes block independent
cinemas from showing box-office hits till the multiplexes
have wrung them dry. This system leaves little room, for
example, for the avant-garde Korean films that can still be
seen in Paris.

McChesney does not mention the fact that there used to
be numerous cinemas showing films in foreign languages
to immigrant populations. When I was a boy, the nearby
German neighborhood of Yorkville still had a cinema
showing only films in German, as did cinemas in Milwaukee
and other immigrant centers. Goebbels' insistence that the
German film industry continue to produce lavish musical
comedies paid off abroad as well as domestically. Before
the Second World War, America had been Germany's first
export market.

As times changed, each immigrant community developed its own infrastructure. For a while, New York and
other cities had numerous Chinese-language cinemas,
though the mainstream press paid no attention to them.
Now these have been largely replaced by the cheap DVDs
coming from Asia; there are still a few Hindi-language
cinemas.

But the independent American movie houses have not
had the same influx of new customers as houses catering
to immigrant audiences. The contrast with France is striking here. There is only one independent not-for-profit

---

1   New York: The New Press, 2000.

cinema in New York, though there are still several struggling to survive as for-profit screens. The Film Forum, to which I have gone faithfully for many years, is a unique success story. Started in 1970 with fifty folding chairs, it now has an impressive 250,000 customers a year, a gross of over $44 million and a staff of fifty-nine. Sixty-four percent of its income comes from ticket sales, the rest from donations and foundation support.

One would expect each city to have supported at least one such not-for-profit independent. But the Sundance Institute has identified only about seventy such cinemas and most of them are not in the big cities. Nor are many of them in major university towns. Instead, the kind of highbrow current releases that one would expect in many decent movie houses are shown at the Loft in Tucson, the Grand in Tacoma, and Cinema Inc. in Raleigh. The exception is the Grand Illusion in Seattle, showing a mix of experimental and classic movies that resemble the French *a and e* programs, and it has all of seventy seats, manned by a volunteer staff.

In a country that still is as addicted to film as the US, with record ticket sales in recent years, it is puzzling that the choice offered to moviegoers is so limited. It would not be difficult for most universities to run or subsidize a not-for-profit cinema, as the University of California does with its Pacific Film Archive. Given the fact that the Museum of Modern Art in New York has long run what is the equivalent of America's *cinemathèque*, a film library, one could expect other museums and even libraries to develop equivalent facilities. In smaller towns where movie houses are an endangered species, people might even want to consider municipal ownership of not-for-profit cinemas.

To be sure, the widespread availability of DVDs has given movie lovers an obvious alternative. These discs certainly accounted for the death of the hundreds of pornographic movie houses that used to exist. But those movies appealed to solitary viewers, happy to have their film at home.

There is still a considerable public of those wanting the experience of viewing a film with others, whether they are fans of current blockbusters or the 250,000 people who go to the Film Forum every year. Clearly it is unrealistic to expect a national tax on movie tickets, such as the French have imposed, to help independent filmmakers as well as art houses—Hollywood's lobbying power is notorious and effective. But that does not mean that some measures, even local and institutional support, could not be developed to create independent cinemas. A tiny local sales tax on movie tickets or even on DVD sales would suffice to create a small not-for-profit independent in most cities.

Even large universities, such as NYU, that have substantial and very profitable film schools do not plow back some of their income into helping create and maintain not-for-profit art houses. Their alumni might be willing to pressure these universities to invest the small amounts that would be needed to place a cinema in one of the auditoriums. As the Film Forum's figures show, the amount that is needed is not enormous, and the survival of the not-for-profit movie houses in smaller cities, cited above, is encouraging.

The historic success of DVD rentals, and the developing technology for downloading these directly to one's television or computer, shows once again that American technological advances encourage individualistic responses, rather than communal ones. But the movie-going experience has been an essential part of the culture for a century. It is a shame to see it kidnapped by those who want to offer only the most profitable blockbusters. The European example, in particular that of Norway, shows that there are other, far more satisfying alternatives that we could at least consider.

until the competition was gradually killed off, after which the chains raised prices. Less than twenty years ago, in 1991, the American Booksellers Association, which serves the independent bookstores, had 5,200 members. In 2005, their number was down to 1,700, roughly a third of that, and is even lower now. Today the book chains are complaining that the large discount stores, like Wal-Mart, are doing the same thing to them, offering books like Harry Potter at a loss in order to lure customers into their stores. In England, the large discounters were offering Harry Potter books for a pound apiece, roughly a twentieth of the "suggested" price. The lawsuits attempted by the independents to stop these unfair practices have not succeeded in the English-speaking world, where opposition to any fixed price continues to fail in the world of books, though not in prescription drugs and many other fields.

It is telling that the French supermarkets, which account for roughly 20 percent of all book sales, are responsible for a third of sales of all children's books, 30 percent of comics, and 75 percent of Harlequin romances, in spite of the *loi Lang*.[1] These sales, along with books published primarily for their customers, such as cookbooks, probably do not siphon off income from the independents. But the supermarket chains do take away many of the best-seller sales that the independents would have made, along with reference works that are put into the shopping cart with the back-to-school specials. One large French independent bookseller complained that he had not sold a single dictionary since a Carrefour supermarket opened outside his town.

---

1   Prosper, *Édition, l'envers du décor.*

Even so, because of the *loi Lang*, the situation in France is much healthier than that in America. Similar laws exist in several European countries: Spain, Greece, Austria, and Portugal. Four others have obtained the same results through private agreements: Germany, Denmark, Holland, and Luxembourg. Overall, France has a better stock of good independent bookstores than Italy, England, and Russia. Only Germany has more. The French stores depend on a culture that still values them and on the commitment of the booksellers and their staffs, who for the most part are badly underpaid. Yet there is a system of support that matters and is worth describing. It is a model for other countries, even though its future depends on political decisions at the national as well as regional level. France has some 900 bookstores considered to be at the highest level of quality, stores with an excellent stock and trained personnel, and 3,874 stores at the second level. These numbers are relatively stable, though there is the growing problem of the aging of the store owners, many of whom will be retiring in the coming years, about which more later. In Germany, the book trade association lists an astonishing 8,000 bookstores, though this includes those selling used books. I once asked Cultural Minister Michael Naumann, a former publisher, what would happen to these stores if the German equivalent of the *loi Lang* were repealed. He answered that they would lose a third of the new-book stores overnight.

In France, moreover, there has developed over the years a substantial structure to help both existing and future bookstores survive and grow. Again, the innovations involved could serve as models for other countries. The most original of them, ALDEC, was started in 1988 by four publishers—Gallimard, Le Seuil, La Découverte, and Les Éditions de Minuit, whose head, Jerome Lindon, a longtime champion of independent stores and of the *loi Lang*, led the effort. Lindon had studied the sales history of a 1985 novel, *La Salle de Bain*, by one of his most promising young authors, Jean-Philippe Toussaint, and discovered that independent stores had sold the book well even before reviews had appeared (an experience that many other publishers have told me they shared).

French publishing was badly affected by discount wars during the 1970s. The *loi Lang*, passed in 1982, helped somewhat for the first two years, though sales in the independent bookstores were still tricky for several years thereafter. (At the start of the Sarkozy government, in 2008, trial balloons were sent up to see if the *loi Lang* might be repealed. At this writing, these unhappy efforts seem to have fizzled out.) So Lindon and the others considered the question of how these crucial independent and literary stores might best be helped. The four publishers created ADELC, which stands for the Association pour le développement de la librairie de création, pledging to fund it with 0.15 percent of their annual sales. Twenty other mainly independent publishers and, surprisingly, the major book club, France Loisirs, soon joined them. The book club's more substantial help, along with government aid, gave the group the funds they needed to begin their program of loans to bookstores. It is only within the last three years that one of the conglomerates, Editis, decided to join the group, though La Découverte, one of its holdings, had been among the founders. The Hachette group has never joined. But without the help of the absent conglomerates, ADELC has raised a total of some 23,000,000 euros, which it has distributed to more than 380 bookstores, not just in France but also in France's overseas territories. The money is given in the form of interest-free loans and can be used for general support, moving stores, or buying up stores being left behind by aging proprietors, an increasingly important task—in 2008, the Ministry of Culture gave ADELC two million euros to help with that alone. The Île-de-France regional council added 500,000 euros this year to help its local bookstores, most of which are in Paris.

French government help has always been a very important part of this overall effort, not only when it provided start-up funds but even now, when close to half of ADELC's annual budget comes from the Centre Nationale du Livre. ADELC is, in effect, what is known in America as a public–private partnership, a way of funneling public money through an independent group of experts who can be counted on to make professional, apolitical decisions. Because of these considerable resources, as the trade journal *Livres Hebdo* calculated in March 2009, a third of all the independent bookstores that they list among the top 400 have been helped—although, as we have seen, the amount of money involved is but a fraction of what has been given to the cinemas, where all qualified recipients are helped every year.

ADELC prides itself on the rigor with which it awards its loans, and the aid and advice it gives recipients. Certainly it is very useful to have a staff of professionals able to talk frankly with bookstore owners and assess their needs. The regional authorities have also made a point of offering technical advice. This has been particularly needed to help the independent bookstores prepare for their long-awaited coordinated Web site, which will allow all of them to compete with Amazon. The various governmental entities I've described are also involved in making sure that this new network is able to handle digitized books, when these inevitably hit the market. But other governments have decided to try to give blanket help, even though of a more modest kind. A pioneer in this respect has been the region of Poitou-Charentes, which has budgeted 1.5 million euros over three years to help its independent "cultural" bookstores—stores that make 40 percent of their sales from backlist titles, have trained help, etc. Each of these stores in the region receives 15,000 euros a year, enough to help pay the salary of a qualified sales clerk. (When *The Business of Books* first came out in Italy, a bill was proposed in the Chamber of Deputies using similar criteria, to lower the taxes on such stores. Alas, the bill failed.) The region of Burgundy also offers substantial aid to independent booksellers: close to 40,000 euros to buy and stock new stores as well as to get needed Internet support. These are grants, as opposed to ADELC's loans. Overall, the regions now control a full half of France's cultural expenditures, allocating some 5 billion euros a year. The proportions are similar in the United Kingdom, though the amounts are much smaller, totaling roughly half the amount spent in France.

As was mentioned at the start of this chapter, towns and even villages in every country, including the US, could also subsidize the rents of their bookstores, or even buy out the location and rent it back, in order to keep the stores in a central place, as has been done with some of the *a et e* cinemas. But clearly the most effective help would come from giving bookstores the kind of more general aid now given to these cinemas, as described above. The sum involved need not be as high as the cinemas' annual 10 million, but it can be strongly argued that bookstores play the same cultural role as these local movie houses. Indeed, they are the most effective way of informing people about the best new books and introducing new and, at times, difficult authors. Increasingly, they also bring in authors to speak, and they serve as de facto cultural centers. In traveling around France and the US, I have been stuck by how loyal and interested the bookstore audiences are and how useful it is, in these days of the mass media, to actually have places where people can get together and exchange ideas. (In some American cities, the bookstores have an event nearly every night, for example, Powell's in Portland, taking on a social and cultural role that should have been that of the local libraries.)

Another interesting idea has been proposed by Christian Ryo, of Lire en Bretagne, one of France's many publicly funded organizations devoted to promoting reading. He suggests that bookstores could work closely with local libraries and open sales counters in them. This is something that has been done in museums throughout France without arousing any protest. Such a program should be organized to help the small local bookstores, not the major national chains, and could easily be arranged on a municipal level.

There is the point that although many bookstores barely make a profit, they are nearly all formally for-profit enterprises. The average annual profit for the smaller stores, those whose book sales total less than 300,000 euros a year, is 0.6 percent.[2] The larger ones, selling over 2 million euros' worth of books a year, manage to make all of 2 percent, far less than other kinds of shops. A few of the best-known bookstores certainly make money. But there is no doubt that all of the independents, whatever their size, render expensive services to the community that the supermarkets (which sell as many books as the independents) and the chains do not. The independents do not concentrate on a limited number of current best sellers, but also have

---

2   Prosper, *Éditions, l'envers du décor.*

a decent selection of older titles; hence the criteria established by Poitou-Charentes. They pay their staff substantially more than their larger competitors and count on them to actually read some of their books and advise their customers. When visiting Dialogues, an impressive bookstore in Brest, I asked what effect this advice could have on sales. For example, they had been recommending Tanguy Viel's novel *Paris-Brest*; how many copies had they been able to sell? To my astonishment, I was told 2,000, more than the New Press had been able to sell of his work in all of the United States.

Other services I have described, such as authors' visits and public discussions, may help establish links with customers, but they rarely bring in enough extra income even to cover the costs of local ads for the event or of inviting the guest writer to dinner. With the help of its publishers, France has recently developed criteria for the better independent bookstores that allow them to have a *labelle*, which lowers some of the taxes the bookstores pay and can open the way to additional help. This is certainly one of the French reforms that could easily be applied in the US, the UK, and other countries.

Following the pattern of assistance given the *a et e* cinemas, aid to bookstores could be based on clear criteria, helping to make good the income lost through the costs of adding these special services. (The large stores take far less risk when they stock not just the current best sellers but also the basic back-to-school items that have made the "cultural" departments of the supermarkets their second most profitable area.) As with the *a et e* cinemas, the amount of aid could be based on the actual activities of each store, their usefulness to the locality, their outreach programs, and so on. It is hard to tell how much stores would eventually depend on this help in their annual plans. Clearly those in Poitou-Charentes know they have some assured grants. But in helping the small bookstores, we are not dealing with a bunch of ruthless capitalists who will invent unrealistic demands. It ought to be possible to see what help is needed for the stores to survive and even to thrive, as has been done with the cinemas.

Unfortunately, with bookstores there is no readily available sum such as the money that comes from the tax on movie tickets. But the amounts involved are not enormous, in any country, and suitable sources for them should not be difficult to find. Just as the French tax TV ads to help the film industry, the source of new taxes to aid bookstores does not have to be directly related to books. Compared to the 700 million euros the Italian government has just given the newspapers—discussed in my chapter on "Saving the Press"—something like 1 percent of that sum would make an important difference, giving a country's best bookstores on a national scale at least what has been done regionally in Poitou-Charentes.

There are also numerous administrative changes that could help bookstores sell to local libraries or to schools. There, France and other European countries are mired in the neoliberal policies dictated by the European Union, aimed at removing any advantage that might be given through a local source. But there is some distance between preferential treatment given to Airbus or to a national airline and allowing a small-town bookstore sell to the local library. Hopefully, in view of the current economic crisis, it will be possible to establish some minimal sums to implement local initiatives wherever they exist. This is hardly protectionism à la Sarkozy, but simply reasonable limits applied to the open-ended international competition insisted upon by Brussels, which is governed by rules that clearly favor the larger multinational enterprises.

In the United States and in the United Kingdom, local schools, universities, and libraries could easily funnel their purchases through the remaining independent bookstores. Unfortunately, in recent years, Barnes & Noble has been able to take over key American university bookstores, like the Harvard and Yale coops. These shortsighted decisions could still be reversed. At the least, course adoptions could be encouraged from the independent bookstores, as Columbia University in New York has done with one of the few remaining independents in its area, Book Culture. No governmental intervention is needed here, though local governments could help public schools and libraries if they felt that maintaining independents mattered to their civic culture.

France has already gone a long way toward helping its booksellers. Few other countries enjoy the range of private and governmental aid described in this chapter. But in spite of this, the crucial last link in the book chain could still use more support. It would not cost much to provide. As with all the solutions suggested in this book, the effectiveness of these programs will depend on the political choices that are made in implementing them, in France and elsewhere. There is no such thing as a free market in the fields of culture. The key decisions are political, whether at the national or local level.

5

The Future of the Press

The decline of newspapers, and to a lesser degree of magazines, has been the subject of widespread debate in both the United States and France for years now. Can newspapers survive as money-making entities? Is the present system, faced with the competition of the Internet and other electronic media, reaching the end of its era, which began in the eighteenth century? In both countries, there is no question that the readership of newspapers has fallen, along with their advertising revenues, leading critics to predict their eventual demise. Two texts published this year have aptly summarized these arguments, and I will cite both of them. In the US, Robert McChesney and another noted writer on the press, John Nichols, coauthored a long article in *The Nation* called "The Death and Life of Great American Newspapers"[1] which has since been expanded into a book called *The Death and Life of American Journalism.*[2] The French journalist Bernard Poulet, known for his excellent history of *Le Monde*, recently published a book called *La*

---

[1] Robert McChesney and John Nichols, "The Death and Life of Great American Newspapers," *The Nation*, April 6, 2009.
[2] New York: Nation Books, 2010.

fin des journaux et l'avenir de l'information,[3] which made strikingly similar arguments, using examples from both the United States and from Europe.

The situation is certainly more dramatic in the United States. There, in the past few years, a number of leading papers have fallen into bankruptcy, including the *Chicago Tribune* and the *Los Angeles Times*, parts of the Tribune Company purchased in 2007 by a notorious Chicago real estate speculator, Samuel Zell, and the *Minneapolis Star Tribune* and the *Philadelphia Inquirer*. Zell's purchase of the two most important papers outside the East Coast is a case study in financial desperation. Zell, a self-proclaimed "grave dancer," had made his billions buying badly indebted real estate and using extremely complex financial maneuvers to make money from it. Some months after Zell's purchase of the papers, *The New Yorker* ran a long profile of Zell, which an outside observer would have turned to expecting a detailed warning about what his latest venture would mean for the papers themselves.[4] But, astonishingly, the magazine praised Zell's exploits, lauding his financial wizardry. Not surprisingly, Zell's attempts to use the papers' debts to finance new backing soon failed. His insistence on continual staff cuts demoralized his employees without making up for the underlying weakness of his financial position as owner. Both papers ended up filing for bankruptcy; they are still being published, but their future is far from secure. Other newspapers have actually closed down, like Denver's venerable daily *The Rocky Mountain News*. Others are threatening to do so, including the *San Francisco Chronicle*,

---

3   Paris: Gallimard, 2009.
4   Connie Bruck, "Rough Rider," *The New Yorker*, November 12, 2007.

the *Seattle Times*, the *Chicago Sun Times*, and the *Newark Star Ledger*.

Even the relatively healthy papers are cutting enormous numbers of staff. Even before the Zell takeover, two editors and a publisher of the *Los Angeles Times* had resigned rather than implement the cuts that were asked of them. Ultimately, 500 of 1,100 employees were eliminated, in response to these earlier demands and then to Zell's profit-preserving pressures. Similarly, the *Baltimore Sun* has gone from 400 journalists to 150, the *Philadelphia Inquirer* from 600 to half that number, the *San Francisco Chronicle* from 500 to 200.[5] Both foreign bureaus and local reporting have been drastically slashed. Increasingly, there is far less coverage of the activities of the local state legislatures, an area of government known for its high level of corruption and where the local press was a crucial critic and counterforce. In 2008, 16,000 newspaper jobs were cut throughout the United States, an incredible number, and a further 10,000 were lost in the first half of 2009.[6] At the start of 2009, still a time of serious recession in the US, the American newspaper industry saw a drop in sales of $2.6 billion, with copy sales falling 10.6 percent. This comes to 44 million fewer copies sold per day, the highest percentage drop since the 1940s. The worst factor has been the decline of ads, down 16.6 percent in 2008 and an astonishing further drop of 28 percent by the end of September 2009. The *San Francisco Chronicle*'s weekday circulation fell 25.8 percent, to less than half the circulation it enjoyed six years ago. Other papers, like

---

5   Leonard Downie, Jr. and Michael Schudson, "The Reconstruction of American Journalism," *Columbia Journalism Review*, October 19, 2009, 17.
6   Richard Pérez-Peña, "US Newspaper Circulation Falls 10%," *New York Times*, October 27, 2009, B3.

the *Newark Star-Ledger* and the *Dallas Morning News*, fell 22 percent. *USA Today*, once the largest daily, fell 17.1 percent, partly due to declining occupancy rates in hotels, where many of its papers are distributed. Clearly, the general recession had a domino effect on the press, in addition to the press's own losses.

Even the *New York Times* is in serious difficulties, losing 7.3 percent of its readers after increasing its price by a third in 2009. Although the paper had refused to cut jobs until 2008, it finally gave in and eliminated 100 positions in the spring of that year and another 100 in the fall of 2009, though it assured its readers that it was not firing anyone in either the overseas or Washington bureaus. Its latest figures show that this "deep cost cutting" increased its net income, allowing the company "to make a modest $19.9 million profit for the year, compared with a loss of $57.8 million" the previous year.[7] The *Times* stated that in 2009 it had cut operating costs by an amazing $475 million, 17.1 percent. This involved cuts in benefits and salaries, closing a distributor, and getting rid of its classical music station, WQXR, now merged with the formerly city-owned not-for-profit WNYC. These losses had led the paper, amazingly, to threaten to shut down the venerable *Boston Globe*, which the *Times* bought in 1993. But it pulled back from that decision after forcing the *Globe*'s unions to accept major cuts worth $20 million.

Clearly, the American situation is dire. But it is a crisis that has been developing for many years. Advertising revenue has been declining since the 1950s: print journals began losing clients to television well before the Internet became

---

7　　Richard Pérez-Peña, "Times Company Reports Profit for Quarter and Year," *New York Times*, February 10, 2010, B5.

a competitor. From 1990 on, newspaper income from ads declined from 26 percent of all media to around 10 percent this year.[8] The circulation figures show a similar decline. Poulet quotes a study by Richard G. Picard showing that daily papers in America sold roughly 54,000,000 copies in 1950, and that figure had increased to only 54,600,000 by 2004, when the population had nearly doubled—a proportional decline of 48 percent, even before the current crisis. (About the same number of newspapers are sold each day in Japan, a country with a population of 125,000,000, roughly a third that of the United States.) Both the debate about the press's decline and the facts underlying it have led to widespread pessimism about the press's future. A public opinion poll in May 2009, recently cited in *USA Today*, found that 65 percent of Americans think that newspapers will no longer exist ten years from now. Younger readers were even more pessimistic. Eighty-three percent of readers 18–29 were not willing to give papers even as much as a decade.

The weekly news magazines *Time*, *Newsweek*, and *US News & World Report*, once the bulwark of information for those not reading a daily paper, have also shown a decline, from 42 million readers in 1988 to 31 million in 2004, a loss of 11,000,000 readers. These figures are not unrelated to an increasing lack of content. It is worth noting that the British weekly the *Economist* is holding steady at a million copies, many of them sold in America. Its pages are far fuller of information than those of its American competitors, who have increasingly used color photographs and fluff in an attempt to keep their readers,

---

8 McChesney and Nichols, *The Death and Life of American Journalism*, 33.

the success of *People* magazine having influenced them along with the rest of the press.

American viewership of the evening news programs has also both aged and declined. It is embarrassing to note the unending commercials for false teeth and heart medications that constantly interrupt these broadcasts. It is hard to escape the feeling that the remaining audience will not be there for long. While 229 per thousand watched these programs a little more than a decade ago, in 2007 that number was 98 per thousand, completing an overall drop of 58 percent over the past quarter century.

The figures for France are not much better. There, newspaper sales have also declined dramatically, as have ad revenues. *Le Figaro*, long one of the country's most prosperous papers, lost a third of its ads between 2003 and 2007, with major ad revenue falling from 120 million euros to 80 million and income from its small classified ads plunging even more precipitously, from 97 million euros to 25 million in the same period. *Le Monde*, likewise, has suffered a very sharp drop, from 100 million euros in 2001 to just half that in 2008. In the 1970s, ads represented 60 percent of *Le Monde*'s income; now that figure is barely 20 percent.

Overall French circulation of the national—that is, the Paris—press has dropped at a similar rate, from 3.8 million in 1974 to exactly half, 1.9 million, in 2007. The decline is similar to that in the US, but occurring over a shorter period. (On the other hand, if one includes all the provincial papers, the total is a healthier 7 million.) As with other print media, there has been a steady decline in the number of young readers: 59 percent of adolescent readers over 15 read a paper in 1967, down to only 34 percent in 2005—a problem that exists in most Western countries. None of the major Paris dailies reaches 400,000. *Le Monde* is first at 340,000; the next two, *Le Figaro* and *Le Parisien*, come in at around 330,000. In 1960, the popular *France-Soir* sold over a million copies a day. On the other hand, it is worth noting that *La Croix* is able to remain in the black with only 100,000 faithful purchasers, in part because of substantial government help (a point that I will discuss in more detail later). The situation in Germany is somewhat better. The Bertelsmann conglomerate has seen the circulation of its papers go from 31.4 million readers in 1997 to 26 million a decade later, a loss, but a much less severe one.

In England, too, the figures show a decline in readership, though primarily among the tabloids—Britain's mass-market papers are hardly comparable to the more classically serious European journals. It is amusing to look at a London newsstand, the British papers all splashed with large headlines and huge color photographs and their continental cousins looking positively nineteenth-century in their restraint. The tabloids' news content is minimal, and their numerous pin-up photographs may have suffered more from the proliferation of pornography on the Internet than from competition from other news media. Possibly their readers, who are largely working class, have become better educated and more sophisticated. Still, the *News of the World*, the Sunday scandal sheet that typified the worst in English journalism and that sold some 8 million copies in the 1950s, now sells fewer than 3 million. The *Sun*, the tabloid that first made Rupert Murdoch's fortune in Britain, sold under 3 million copies in 2007, down from 4.3 million in 1988. All of the other papers are losing readers, too, though not as dramatically. The *Sunday Times*, with 1.1 million, lost 5 percent of them in 2007. The more serious broadsheets (with the exception of the very profitable *Telegraph*), such as the *Guardian* and the *Independent*, are in financial difficulty, their sales being similar to their Parisian counterparts.

The *Guardian* provides a particularly interesting case, since for years it and its Sunday edition, the *Observer*, have belonged to the not-for-profit Scott trust. The trust could afford some losses on the *Guardian*, since it also owns a highly profitable monthly, *Motor Trends*. But like all such specialized journals, *Motor Trends'* advertisers have been fleeing to the Web. Last year, 2009, was a hard one for the *Guardian*, with losses of some 90 million pounds, which forced it to sell off its lucrative local paper, the *Manchester Evening News*. Yet the *Guardian* refuses to charge for its Web site, the most popular in England with 37 million visits a month, considering it to be a public service. However, the paper is proving to be ingenious in developing new sources of income. The latest is providing subscribers with the paper's content on their iPhones. So far, they have 100,000 subscribers for this, each paying a modest 2.39 pounds a month—little more than the cost of two issues. The Guardian says it is working on other such ideas, though whether these can make up for the grave losses brought by the recession is unclear.[9]

So the future of two of England's leading papers—and of its most independent ones—remains at risk. Interestingly, the *Financial Times* is the profitable exception, selling 450,000 copies worldwide, with an increase of 2.5 percent last year. But half of those sales are overseas, a parallel to the success of the *Economist* in the US

---

9 "Au Royaume-Uni, le 'Guardian' cherche un modèle rentable entre le journal papier, l'Internet et l'iPhone," *Le Monde*, March 16, 2010.

and elsewhere.[10] The one paper to see a major increase in circulation has been the *Evening Standard*, since its owner, the Russian Alexander Lebedev, recently took the gamble of making it a free paper, which raised the tabloid's circulation from 230,000 to 600,000.[11] Whether this will make the paper more profitable has yet to be seen, but as in France, it shows that the readership of traditional papers can still be substantially increased.

On the Internet, English-language publications enjoy a great advantage, and this has allowed the better British papers to establish a very successful Web presence. The *Telegraph* and the *Guardian* each receive 18 million visitors a month, figures similar to those for the *New York Times*; by contrast, *Le Monde* receives only 3,500,000. Many of the English-speaking papers' Web site readers come from abroad, just as for years a substantial number of the *Manchester Guardian Weekly*'s readers lived in India and in the US.

But clearly the printed press in Western Europe and the US is in serious difficulty. This has not happened overnight and is not solely due to competition from the Internet, though *Le Figaro*'s loss of classified ads clearly is. What is astonishing is that this long-term decline should not have alarmed the press much sooner. Yet, until very recently, American investors expected a return of 26 percent from their newspaper stocks, and staffs were cut and coverage limited to provide such income, even though these very measures were bound to lose readers. The most notorious example was the decision to sell the Knight Ridder newspapers. Wall Street experts would argue that this was but

---

10   These figures are all from Poulet.
11   Paul Roche, "L' 'Evening Standard' à zéro penny," *Le Monde*, October 6, 2009.

the tip of the iceberg and that it was high time to move out of an industry which had once been exceptionally profitable but which was now clearly on the decline.

And yet, failing to realize that they were on the edge of a financial precipice, newspaper owners went on very expensive shopping sprees in the 1990s, buying into other media, as did the *New York Times*, whose debts now total an incredible $1.1 billion, more than the firm's total worth. This is partly thanks to its decision to build a lavish new skyscraper in the middle of Manhattan, designed by Renzo Piano, which cost the paper some $600,000,000, creating more than half that debt, when its old and admittedly dilapidated headquarters could well have been used for many more years. Many on the staff now regret a decision that may well cost them their jobs in the future, and the paper has already leased parts of the building to other tenants to recoup some of this unwise investment. The *Times* has also been forced to negotiate a loan from the Mexican telecommunications billionaire Carlos Slim, who has agreed to lend it $250,000,000 against a warrant on 15.9 million shares, which would make him the largest stockholder after the founding family. This is something the *Times* long sought to avoid, being already engaged in a constant battle with some of its minority shareholders, who are dying to cut staff and increase the paper's meager profits.

The most dramatic example of indebtedness among European papers is Spain's *El Pais*, reported to owe well over 2 billion euros after its purchase of Spanish television stations. *Le Monde*, following the dubious advice of the financier Alain Minc, bought up an impressive array of other media properties, including bookstores, many of which it has since had to sell. *Le Monde* does depend heavily on the circulation and profits of the most successful of its purchases, the weekly cultural magazine *Telerama*, whose circulation is much higher than *Le Monde*'s own. The crisis has led to feverish governmental attempts, particularly in France and Italy, to inject money into the printed press, about which more later. But the basic problems have been around for a long time and remained unaddressed in both countries until very recently.

Several questions need to be asked. First of all, is this the inevitable fate of newspapers throughout the world? Curiously, Poulet does not ask this question, though the figures in both Europe and Asia are striking. Japan is the most interesting case. Its leading newspaper, the *Yumiori Shimbun*, sells over 14 million copies per day. Its closest competitor, the *Asahi Shimbun*, sells over 12 million. Four other dailies have sales of between four million and five million copies. These are serious papers, not at all like the British tabloids, the closest match the West could offer in terms of high sales. In 2004, the total daily Japanese newspaper sales of 53 million were actually up from 52.8 the previous year, though they have slipped by 32 percent in the decade as a whole (as opposed to a 15 percent decline in the US). Overall sales are 624 papers per thousand persons, two and a half times greater than the US figure, with more than one paper delivered to every household. Newspaper employment in Japan has remained largely stable. Ad revenue in 2004 was up slightly, though the Internet has begun to have the usual effect, siphoning off some of those ads.

Overall, 74 of the world's top 100 dailies are published in Asia, and their total circulation in 2007 was up by 2.6 million. The highest increase has been in China, with 107 million copies sold daily, and in India, with 99 million. Obviously these last two countries are benefiting from the rise of a middle class and that class's greater share of income. But those explanations do not apply to Japan, which is caught up in a serious recession and has long been addicted to electronic media and its diversions.

One might think that these figures would intrigue our French and American colleagues, or at least that they would have taken notice by now of the impressive numbers from Norway. But Western critics, indeed all of Western media, are amazingly centered on their own countries and unused to looking beyond their borders. All newspapers now have media pages. One might have expected at least one article on the Asian phenomena. But critical coverage of the media remains stolidly provincial, giving endless space to national problems but not a word to the rest of the world. These comparative data do not suggest that the crisis in France and in the US is not real. Clearly it is, and competition from the Internet is a major factor, more in advertising than in readership, as 96 percent of the time Americans devote to newspapers is spent reading their printed form.[12]

But before discussing these statistics, we should ask to what degree the newspapers themselves have been responsible for their declining readership. As I've stated, the gradual decline in circulation and, in the US, the constant pressure to maintain unrealistically high profits, have resulted in less coverage, fewer pages, and fewer foreign correspondents. In recent years the total number of the latter, globally, is reported to have fallen from 2,500 to 250. Many of the important American papers, like the *Baltimore Sun*, have shut their last foreign bureau. And since the TV networks decided some years ago that their news operations should be treated as independent profit centers,

---

12   Michael Massing, "A New Horizon for the News," *New York Review of Books*, September 24, 2009.

foreign coverage on television has also greatly declined. The consequences of all these changes were dramatically demonstrated by the American coverage, or noncoverage, of the war in Iraq. As I've discussed in *Le Controle de la Parole*, it was far easier for the American government to systematically lie to the press when there were far fewer reporters covering what was being said about its actions in other countries. There are no figures on this, but I suspect that the decline of newspaper readership in America is due in part to the general disillusionment that resulted from this failure. I do not believe that newspapers lost readers, or evening TV broadcasts their viewers, during the Vietnam War, which was eventually—though not initially—covered thoroughly and truthfully.

An equally important weakness, which cannot be attributed to governmental pressure, was the inability of the press as a whole to predict the current economic crisis. There were many impressive economists who pointed out that the market was on a perilous course, but they were not listened to. The Friedman ideology, which insists that the market can do no wrong, prevailed in the press as it did in the universities. Had the *Times* and other papers discussed the danger in time, they might have affected governmental policy. Or, at the very least, they would have given their readers the impression that the press was independent and writing critically on these crucial issues. Its failure to do so has, I am sure, contributed to its readers' loss of faith in it.

The French press, meanwhile, is caught in a vicious circle similar to the situation in the US: financial problems force newspapers to fire more and more journalists; and afterward the papers must print less news on fewer pages. *Le Monde*, for instance, has not had a reporter in Kabul and is generally spread thin in Asia, where much of the current important world news is breaking. There is also a strong French tradition of self-censorship where the government is concerned. The press avoids the leaks that have been red meat for American papers. As a result, the weekly *Canard Enchaîné*, which thrives on publishing the leaks its colleagues ignore, has a far greater circulation than they do. With roughly 550,000 copies sold each week, it is solidly profitable and can afford to hire some of the journalists let go by the more respectable papers.

Whether better coverage would lure younger readers is difficult to ascertain. Certainly one of the major problems facing these media is the aging of their constituency. Young people, influenced by the Internet, text messages, blogs, and Twitter, seem alienated from the traditional media and far more interested in self-defined social networks like Facebook than in the real outside world. They are less comfortable with the conventional news media, whether printed or electronic. All statistics agree on this, and it is beyond the scope of this book to try to analyze the generational differences that seem to be at work throughout the West. I have seen no serious analysis of the relation of the content of the media to the growing lack of interest among the young.

Still, it is important to note that a major factor that is cited in the decline of paid newspapers in the West is the proliferation of free papers, which are read overwhelmingly by the young. In France, the circulation of the leading free paper, *20 Minutes*, 800,000, is double that of *Le Monde*. Though these free papers are now also in crisis because of the general reduction of ads caused by the global recession, the fact remains that they are enormously successful, even if they are no longer as profitable. The Swedish-based Metro chain has a hundred free dailies throughout the world, including a very popular New York version. This shows that younger readers are perfectly willing to read printed papers, even if only in shorter, snappier versions of the traditional press. Could the traditional papers have reached out more effectively to younger readers, and how? By altering either form or content?

Or did the free papers work simply because they were free and fitted in to the younger generation's assumption that news should be given away, whether on the Internet or at the newsstand? The impressive success of the government's recent offer of free newspapers to the young, which I will discuss in the next chapter, reinforces that idea.

Yet the experience of the Paris daily *Liberation* is not encouraging. It has tried desperately to appeal to a younger audience, devoting as much space to subjects of popular culture as to its regular news coverage. However, this has not really helped circulation, and the paper continues to publish at a loss, in spite of having let a large number of its journalists go. (To be fair, a Spanish equivalent, *Publico*, has been launched successfully in recent years, but it contains far more pages and much more news.) Perhaps expecting younger readers to pay for news, given that they have been used to free news on the Internet—and now get it on their cell phones—is a lost cause. But again, we have not seen persuasive efforts by the leading papers to deal with the issues that determine the lives of the young (as opposed to the distractions that are offered them). Were they to deal constantly and concretely with the problems of employment among the young, the effect of governmental policies on their daily lives, and similar issues of immediate interest, they might well capture some younger readers.

There is also the question of appealing to the growing communities of ethnic minorities in these countries. News coverage, both in France and in the US, is solidly white. Though American papers and television stations have been much more successful in recruiting journalists from minority communities, and the BBC stands as a remarkable contrast to others in Europe with its black financial reporters and the like, the actual coverage of the lives of minority groups, both in the US and England, has not been increased to reflect their increasing presence. Having black weather forecasters and Asian-American co-anchors has not changed the way these communities are reported on by American local broadcasters. To take just one example, a 2005 review of more than 12,000 national evening news stories that appeared on CBS, NBC, and ABC revealed that fewer than 1 percent of them were exclusively about Latinos or Latino-related issues—a figure that had gone virtually unchanged for more than a decade, even though Hispanics comprise 14.5 percent of the US population and are the nation's fastest-growing population group.[13]

As is well known, when the Paris banlieues exploded the other year, *Le Monde* had to bring in their one, part-time, reporter of North African background from Lyon to cover the events. That was a classic case of far too little, much too late, since the paper should have been covering these tensions well before they exploded. Whether a paper in Paris could seduce some of the county's 10 percent or more of the country's "immigrant" population is another unanswered question. I am struck whenever I pass the newspaper kiosk at the Belleville metro stop, near my Paris publisher's office, to see the very high stacks of newspapers for sale. But they are not *Le Monde* or even *Liberation*. The

---

13 Juan Gonzalez and Joseph Torres, *White News*, New York: Verso Books, forthcoming.

three very serious looking papers are in Chinese, though they are published in France. When I asked the French kiosk owner how many of them she sold each day, she answered at least 500. A similar phenomenon exists in New York, where my local newsstand in the city's Upper West Side has an impressive display of Chinese- and Korean-language papers. New York has radio stations broadcasting 24 hours a day in Mandarin, and overall, an impressive 57 million Americans are reached by the ethnic press and radio. This segregation of media helps, of course, to segregate the new immigrants in every country. In France this has contributed to the extraordinary concept of "third-generation immigrants," a phrase and idea in common use there, though unthinkable in other countries.

It can certainly be argued that even if the press were better and more comprehensive, it would still be suffering from the competition of the Internet. There is no question that Internet ad revenues are huge and growing quickly. Poulet cites an American estimate that they will increase by 20 percent a year until 2011 and by then could account for $62 billion, as opposed to $60 billion for the printed press and $86 billion for radio and television, with only a tiny fraction accounted for by the newspapers' own Web sites.[14] In France the numbers, though smaller, are still impressive. The Web represents 20 percent of all ad monies. In 2006, advertisers spent 1.7 billion euros on the Web, as opposed to 7 billion on the press, 6.3 billion on television, and 3.3 billion on radio. But young people are gradually changing their preferences. In 2006, 71 percent of the crucial 18–34 group said they were spending less time watching

---

14   Poulet, 37.

television (and presumably more on the Web). Since young people are the prime target of advertisers, it is not surprising that those advertisers should be shifting their budgets away from media that largely address the older generation. But the particular appeal of ads on the Web is how tightly they can focus on any given audience. The tastes and preferences you show while using the Internet give its owners an individualized profile that can be sold to whatever advertiser seeks to reach you, an enormous advantage over the blanket coverage offered by the traditional media, no matter how large its audience.

In addition to the advertising shift among the media, there is the major, but largely unreported, shift among nations. The American Internet sites are siphoning off an enormous percentage of foreign ad expenditures: 70 percent of European ads are now on American sites, representing some $7 billion in 2007, and another $6 billion came in from Asia.[15] This is something that needs to be considered when discussing Internet profits.

There is no question that the Internet is a major cause, if not the major cause, of the decline of newspaper sales in the countries I've mentioned. Some newspapers, primarily in England, have been able to reach a large number of readers on their Web sites, but very few have been able to raise enough advertising income to make up for the loss of ads in their printed version. A few papers may go back to charging readers for access to their Web sites. The *Financial Times* decided to charge their online readers beginning in August 2009. Faced with a 40 percent decline in profits in the first half of 2009 over 2008, its editors felt such a change was essential. The Web site revenue is accordingly up 30

---

15   Poulet, 51.

percent over the previous year, with some 117,000 subscribers paying $299 a year each. But the *Financial Times* is in an exceptional position. Most of its readers feel they need its information for their own businesses, and I assume they feel free to bill their companies for these expenses. This also may be working for the *Wall Street Journal*, which has 1.1 million subscribers to its Web site, who pay from $100 to $140 a year to get the paper's reports on business and finance. The site as a whole received 12 million hits in April 2009, and the owner, Rupert Murdoch, may well decide to make all of its coverage subject to payment.

But it is doubtful that most readers of other papers would be willing to pay for general content, as in some cases they once did. The few recent attempts to convert free coverage to subscription only do not seem to have paid off. The *New York Times* has so far decided that the potential income from online subscriptions would be smaller than the ad revenue they now get from a far larger audience, though it has decided to charge for some of its coverage—for now, casual use is free, but heavy readers will pay.[16]

In France, former *Le Monde* journalists created a pay-for-use Web site, Mediapart, which after two years has just 15,000 subscribers. This is a third of what is needed to break even, and whether the full amount can be reached has yet to be seen. In the meanwhile, investors in the site are still willing to pour in additional cash.

Many readers are now accustomed to reading the news when they turn on their computer, on the Google page or elsewhere. For the most part, this news is simply taken from the printed press or from the wire services. Eric Schmidt,

---

16 Richard Pérez-Peña, "The Times to Charge for Frequent Access to Its Web Site," *New York Times*, January 20, 2010.

head of Google, has argued that this actually helps the newspapers, by building their audience on the Web and hence
increasing their ad revenue. This argument may have some
validity, but the newspaper Web sites are unable to pay
more than a fraction of the cost of actually producing the
news. The fact remains that the Web is simply cannibalizing
the papers and in some cases changing reading habits, so that
people become satisfied with the brief headlines on the page
they reach when turning on their computer.

This is not to say that the Internet has not been important in conveying news that the newspapers either ignore,
censor, or, increasingly, no longer cover. We have only
to look at the use of the Web after the Iranian election,
when both the Internet and cell phones became the major
dissenting sources of information—and the only way
to get past the limits placed on professional journalists.
(Ironically, the overthrow of the Shah was greatly helped
by an earlier technology: tape-recorded sermons of the
Ayatollah, smuggled in from France.) Equally vital was
the Web's role during the American invasion and occupa-
tion of Iraq, when much of the dissident coverage available in the US was online, but those articles were primarily
taken from the European papers, which had paid to send
their correspondents to cover the events.

The Web has also been invaluable in running other
stories that the press ignored or was afraid to run. There is
no underestimating the potential use of the Web for citizen
action, as was shown by the very successful mobilization of
the Web by the Obama presidential campaign, following
the example of MoveOn.org and other groups that had led
the opposition to Bush's Iraq policies.

Finally, there is the growing use of the Internet to cover
local, even neighborhood, events and politics. More and

more American newspapers are introducing these hyper-local sites, relying heavily on reader involvement for their coverage, though possibly at the cost of no longer having their own trained journalists covering local and state politics, areas that have been among the first targets of staff cuts.[17]

Recent press articles have been full of accounts of these new Web sites and their possible promise. These developments are widely heralded and will doubtless make up for some of the cuts in the traditional newspapers; on the other hand, there is a danger that the rapid proliferation of new sites could end by drowning the would-be reader in endless choices, some of them frivolous.

One Web site has even begun to give cameras to school-children to cover the events in their schools. The lines between Facebook and Twitter and news coverage are becoming increasingly blurred. Although there is much potential value in the discovery of local talent and soliciting of local comment, we may soon reach the point where the overwhelming amount of information and entertainment on the Web becomes self-defeating. The filtering practiced by the traditional press does serve a useful purpose, though certainly it has often been misused. As Google's Eric Schmidt has stated, the Web is also a "cesspool of misinformation," some of it deliberately so. It is increasingly used to convey false claims, as in the US debate on health care, where partisan Web sites played a role, alongside partisan broadcast media, in spreading disinformation, such as the infamous "death panel" scare. It is impossible to know who is writing what and with what motives. The

17   Andy Newman, "Hey Kids, Let's Put on a Blog!", *New York Times*, March 2, 2009.

famous Wikipedia, for instance, has let people write their own biographies, and it is no defense for them to claim that these carry no more errors than the Encyclopedia Britannica, itself hardly a paragon of accuracy. If anything, the Web demonstrates that there is an even greater need for distance, analysis, and expert commentary, which have become increasingly rare. In other words, there is still a real need for the traditional activities of the press.

But it is far from clear what newspapers can do to meet the present challenges. The next chapter will look at the different solutions that have been proposed in recent years.

6

Saving the Press

At the beginning of last year, on January 27, 2009, the *New York Times* ran an op-ed piece that led to a great deal of comment.[1] Its main author, David Swensen, was identified as the author of *Pioneering Portfolio Management*, a reassuring book title. He is the chief investment officer at Yale, which has one of the most successful endowment programs of any American university. Most American banks envied the annual returns that Swensen was able to give his employer. His coauthor on the article, Michael Schmidt, is one of his financial analysts. Yale's endowment, though not the country's largest, is an impressive $22.6 billion, and the interest from this helps defray a large part of its annual operating budget of $2.31 billion. (The rest of the money comes from grants and tuition.) Clearly, Swensen is used to dealing with considerable sums. In this article, he briefly outlines the crisis we have been discussing. Moving newspapers to Web sites, he argues, no matter how successfully, would not generate enough income to support the papers. *The New York Times*, for instance, whose site drew

---

1 Michael Schmidt and David Swensen, "News You Can Endow," *New York Times*, January 27, 2009.

some 20 million users in October 2008, raises only enough Web-based revenue to pay for a fifth of its staff. The obvious solution, he says, is to turn newspapers into not-for-profit institutions, along the lines of universities.

An independent, endowed newspaper would be free from pressures from advertisers and from stockholders alike, he argues, making a point that few others have deigned to consider. How large an endowment would be needed? Without hesitating, Swensen looks at the $200 million a year that the *Times* needs for its reporting and adds a little something extra for overhead (without including the $600 million the *Times* spent on its new building). Figuring an annual income of 5 percent of the capital, Swensen comes up with the figure of $5 billion; less would be needed for smaller papers. By the standards of Yale's multibillion-dollar endowment, this seems a bargain.

But many of those who commented on the article felt it was an unrealistic amount to expect from foundations and individuals, the sources Swensen proposed. The idea of private endowment must have seemed a perfectly natural one to someone in his position. After all, Yale, Harvard, and other American universities raise vast amounts from their alumni every year. It does not seem to have occurred to him that the government could offer any help beyond the tax deductions allowed for all those donations. Nor does he seem aware that the German philosopher Jürgen Habermas published a similar proposal in 2007.[2]

Habermas was confronting an immediate and actual rather than a theoretical problem. The great Munich newspaper *Süddeutsche Zeitung*, flagship of left-of-center

---

2 Jürgen Habermas, "Keine Demokratie kann sich das leisten," *Süddeutsche Zeitung*, May 16, 2007.

journalism in Germany, was faced with an outside take-over. As so often happens with family-owned concerns, the descendants of the paper's founders lacked the funds to keep it going independently and were searching for outside capital. Such help was unlikely to come from sources that would be friendly to the paper's left-leaning editorial policies. Since Germany does not have a tradition of privately endowed universities, nor of vast private foundations, Habermas suggested the logical alternative, that the German government fund an independent endowment. Being a philosopher and not a financial analyst, he did not go into the precise details of how much money would be needed or how it might be allocated. But he put the idea out there, and unfortunately, that is where it stayed. His compatriots were quick to shoot it down, not even giving their most noted philosopher the courtesy of a careful analysis or refutation. It seemed to them a given that because of Germany's Nazi past, such a proposal was out of the question, in spite of the many successful government-funded radio and television stations that had been created after the war. Though *Le Monde* translated his article, the French press likewise did not deem it worthy of further comment.

An indication of the assumptions on the American side of the debate is clearly demonstrated in a report published by the prestigious Columbia University Journalism School in October 2009, tellingly called "The Reconstruction of American Journalism" (note: not of newspapers). The report was written by Leonard Downie, Jr., an official at the *Washington Post*, and Michael Schudson, a professor at the school. The report focuses primarily on the growth of new journalistic Web sites. Its conclusion begins with this startling declaration: "We are not recommending a government bailout of newspapers nor any of the various direct subsidies that governments give newspapers in many European countries, although those subsidies have not had a noticeably chilling effect on newspapers' willingness to print criticisms of these governments. Nor are we recommending direct government financing or control of television networks or stations.

"Most Americans have a deep distrust of direct government involvement or political influence in independent news reporting, a sentiment we share. But this should not preclude government support for news reporting."[3] The authors go on to argue that "the marketplace will determine [which] experiments will ultimately be successful,"[4] though many of the experiments they describe are based on foundation or university funding. Clearly, these strong denials are meant to lead up to the series of modest suggestions the report has to offer, such as indirect forms of governmental help, primarily to broadcasters. The report's authors want to make clear that they are not closet socialists, lest their modest proposals be attacked on the same ground as have so many of President Barack Obama's cautious reforms.

But what is really striking is the report's unwillingness to discuss existing government powers that have been in place since the beginning of broadcasting. The Federal Communications Commission has long had the power to demand that broadcasters show they are "acting in the public interest" in exchange for their use of the airwaves, still the country's principal natural resource. So great were the pressures to develop the resource along these lines in

---

3 Leonard Downie, Jr. and Michael Schudson, "The Reconstruction of American Journalism," *Columbia Journalism Review*, October 19, 2009, 72.
4 Ibid., 74.

the 1930s that, as McChesney reminds us in his *Rich Media, Poor Democracy*,[5] the NBC radio network paid for a full symphony orchestra under the baton of Arturo Toscanini, in addition to many other public service broadcasts. Since the Reagan era's rightward revisions of the FCC directive, these pressures have largely disappeared, and what were once serious attempts at public review of the stations have become pro-forma renewals. There has been a similar change in the implementation of the "equal time" regulation, which is supposed to be applied to all candidates during national elections. This last change has perhaps altered American political life more than any other, since it has led to the frenetic fundraising which characterizes all campaigns and gives the powerful corporations their stranglehold on the political process—something that was made abundantly clear by the many compromises Obama had to make in pushing his plans for health care reform.

The report does not even consider the potential effect of reintroducing a meaningful implementation of public-interest requirements for local and other news broadcasting. Instead, it suggests a series of changes that would increase government funding for the Corporation for Public Broadcasting, the closest thing America has to the European public networks. The authors note that the $400 million that Congress annually appropriates for the CPB is meager compared to other countries' support for public programming: the US spends $1.35 per capita; the UK gives $80 per capita for the BBC and Denmark's and Finland's equivalents get $100. They point out the little known fact that the FCC gets some $7 billion a year from telephone surcharges, which it uses to aid telecom service

5   New York: The New Press, 2000.

in rural areas. They suggest that part of this money could be used to help local news coverage on public radio and television, a helpful and original idea, though one that clearly contradicts the authors' pledge of allegiance to free enterprise. Still, implementation of FCC regulations on private broadcasters, which means the overwhelming majority of stations, would be far more effective.

It seems reasonable to assume that if the United States makes any progress in establishing a program of governmental help, however indirect, it may take the form of the kind of expanded aid to PBS that the report recommends. It is telling that the respected press critic Michael Massing, in a series of articles in the *New York Review of Books*,[6] comes to a similar conclusion. PBS is an accepted part of American media life and has actually expanded its audience during the current crisis, showing a 9 percent increase in 2008, bringing its audience to a total of 20.9 million viewers.[7] Though it, too, has had to cut jobs—77 in 2008—it has been able to survive and grow. Its funds come only partially from the federal government. Forty-three percent comes from its 860 member stations, all of them noncommercial and all depending in turn on listener contributions, which in effect are voluntary fees.

McChesney and Nichols, in their *Death and Life of American Journalism*, also stress the importance of public broadcasting, but as part of a much more ambitious menu of possible indirect government aid. Seeking to place their ideas in the context of American history, they stress the help that was given to the American press at its very beginning. If the government now spent the same percentage

6   "The News About the Internet," August 13, 2009, and "A New Horizon for the News," September 9, 2009.
7   "A New Horizon for the News," 24.

of GDP on media as it did in the 1840s, the press, written and broadcast, would have some \$30 billion at its disposal. Accordingly, the authors make a number of suggestions. Remembering the cheap postage rates that Benjamin Franklin encouraged, they suggest similarly cheap rates for publications with less than 25 percent of their content devoted to advertising and a circulation below 500,000, criteria that cover all journals with any serious content.

They also suggest that everyone receive a \$200 annual tax credit for subscribing to a daily newspaper.[8] This would pay for only a hundred copies of the *New York Times* or forty weeks of its Sunday edition. But they argue that if enough people grouped their donations, for that is what these subscriptions would be considered, that would generate enough revenue to support a local paper or radio station. All media entities in the program would have to be not-for-profit, which worries McChesney and Nichols, since such entities cannot back candidates or specific legislation. But a not-for-profit paper's editorial freedom would be substantial, as it is for such not-for-profit papers as the *St. Petersburg Times*, which according to the *American Journalism Review* "many journalists consider the nation's finest local newspaper."[9] McChesney and Nichols go on to argue that the best of all worlds can be found in the formula of the L3C, or low-profit company—a very new corporate structure, only recognized in five states in the US thus far—that prioritizes the social aims of the company and allows for investment from foundations.[10] In either case, the classic capitalist model would have to be abandoned,

---

8   McChesney and Nichols, "The Death and Life of Great American Newspapers," *The Nation*, April 6, 2009.
9   Quoted, McChesney and Nichols, 177.
10   McChesney and Nichols, 182–90.

which makes good sense for papers that no longer expect to make any profits but raises problems for those like the *New York Times* that have large shareholders who would doubtless be unwilling to give up their considerable holdings.

Among other intriguing ideas that the authors propose is one they adopted from Ken Doctor, author of *Newsonomics*: developing a press equivalent of the privately and publicly funded Teach for America program. Young journalists would be paid $35,000 a year to work on any paper or radio or TV station that will accept them. Establishing 2,500 such posts would cost a mere $90 million a year.[11] And McChesney and Nichols also cite a related suggestion by the late University of Pennsylvania law professor Ed Baker that newspapers be granted a tax credit of up to $45,000 for all journalists employed—a far more expensive proposal, which could cost $3.5 billion annually.[12] They point out that the government now spends $1 billion annually on the Pentagon's propaganda efforts, though it's not clear that this comparison would persuade anyone not already in favor of their ideas.

One of the fascinating historic events that they dig up happened when the idea of public television was first being discussed in the 1960s. The Carnegie Commission, charged with making basic proposals, came close to the European model in proposing an excise tax on the sale of TV sets that would go into a trust fund over which the government would have no control. This would have brought in a sum equivalent to $4 billion in 2009, less than the subsidy provided by the Canadian government to its public media, but still ten times what is now offered by today's US

11   Ibid., 170.
12   Ibid., 188–9.

government.[13] It is fascinating to see that, as with Truman's original proposals for a National Health Insurance in 1948, there was a time when America was able to consider much bolder ideas than it has in recent decades. Of course, once PBS began to broadcast daring exposés, its future was sealed, with Richard Nixon even vetoing its entire budget authorization in 1972.

To pay for the programs they outline, McChesney and Nichols suggest four major sources of funding. The first would be a 7 percent tax on the profits of private broadcasters, which they estimate would bring in $3 billion to $6 billion. Related to this would be a tax on upcoming auctions of the broadcast spectrum, which have been incredibly profitable for these companies. The authors also go back to the Carnegie proposal for a tax on consumer electronics, adding a tax on cell phones. Finally, they argue for a 2 percent tax on advertising, which companies are now able simply to write off as a business expense. All of this together would generate close to $25 billion, they estimate—not enough to pay for all of their proposals, but a good start.[14]

Clearly these ideas are not meant to define the debate but simply to start one. McChesney and Nichols are much more direct in their approach than their colleagues at the Columbia Journalism School, making it clear that they are happy to use the Federal government's taxing powers to help maintain an independent journalism. Whether these ideas will be much listened to during a period of fear and recession is another question. It is unimaginable that the cautious, if not conservative, Obama government would

13   Ibid.,194.
14   Ibid., 210–1.

fight for new taxes of this kind, even indirect ones. But McChesney and Nichols have had the courage to propose a whole agenda that would certainly change the media scene. One can only hope that, in time, their ideas will be debated.

As for the Europe discussion, the conclusion of Poulet's book is in striking contrast to the proposals of the American center as embodied in the Columbia report. Poulet is editor-in-chief of a business magazine, *Expansion*, and he runs through all the possible ways in which newspapers might extend their profit-making activities. He is hopeful about the Web, and even enthusiastic about the growing role of merchandizing—newspapers selling secondary products, such as books, records, and videos, to their readers. It is only at the very end of his text that Poulet notes that there "are services for public education and health, why not imagine a public information service, independent of government . . . The old BBC gives us an interesting other model." But he leaves it at that, whereas I would insist that this is exactly where the argument should begin.

Realistically, the future of the press is probably best described by the grim statistics I've already discussed. Many of the journalists with whom I talk are simply hoping that their papers will last until they reach their retirement age. The shift away from print is already assumed by many to be a certainty. One of the oldest and most respected American newspapers, the *Christian Science Monitor*, has already abandoned its paper edition for the Web. Others are experimenting with dual editions, appearing in print and on the Web.

But the most important questions go beyond form. It is content that matters, and the major role played by the press is one of gathering and filtering the news and also analyzing and commenting on its import. These are the functions that need to be preserved, whatever shape they may take. There is a continuing need for long-form investigative reporting, from whatever source. An interesting proof of this has been furnished by a new journal in France called *XXI*. Started two years ago by a former *Figaro* reporter, Patrick de Saint-Exupéry, and the founder of the publishing house Les Arènes, Laurent Beccaria, the journal's basic assumption is that reporters have been frustrated by their inability to write in-depth articles for the daily press and that readers are equally unhappy about not being able to read them. After two years of sales exclusively in bookstores—which saves on distribution costs— at a relatively high price per copy, 15 euros, *XXI* has established a steady circulation of 45,000, much higher than its founders hoped for (or indeed than I had thought possible when first hearing of their plans). Ironically, *Le Monde* has begun to run excerpts from some of these articles, but this is only a short-term solution, hardly the response that one expects from those who should be originating the articles to begin with.

In the United States, even the *New York Times* has begun to run investigative articles funded by a new not-for-profit, ProPublica, recently established with a grant of $30 million from progressive California billionaires to enable papers to report stories neglected by the mainstream press. The program was launched in 2008 by a former *Wall Street Journal* managing editor, Paul Steiger, and now employs some 36 reporters and editors in fancy new offices in New York. Their stories have helped fill the gap in the press's coverage of numerous key domestic issues, and its articles have appeared in all the nation's leading newspapers. ProPublica won a Pulitzer Prize in 2010. Similar efforts are being made by Politico, the very popular Washington Web site, and the Huffington Post, whose stories are widely picked up, though the site itself has yet to claim that it is profitable. When one looks at the American situation realistically, it seems likely that the decline of the established newspapers will continue and that a new network of local and foundation-sponsored Web sites will complement or even take the place of the existing papers.

A spate of recent articles has welcomed this development, and so has the *Columbia Journalism Review* report. I do not mean to denigrate the good work done by these news sites by pointing out, with Massing, that according to a recent survey, Internet users (who do not represent the entire American public, after all) spent 53 minutes a week reading newspapers online in 2008. Massing hails the increase from 41 minutes in 2007, and this may indeed indicate a trend. Even so, this is less than eight minutes a day, assuming that the habit of Sunday newspaper reading has disappeared for these folks. As an old-fashioned print reader, I find it hard to spend less than an hour on the *New York Times* or *Le Monde*, even on a slow news day. Eight minutes is enough to glance at the headlines and perhaps read one story. What is being lost here may well be the habit of reading, as Web surfers become accustomed to a quick summary, even briefer than that offered on the radio or television. Admittedly, only 3 percent of readers overall get their news on the Web, but these figures should limit the enthusiasm building up over Web news sites as substitutes for the traditional press.

Knowing this, many new foundation-funded organizations are establishing links to the local press. In Chicago, for instance, the MacArthur Foundation has funded a group of former journalists to cover the news in that city and to fill two pages of the *New York Times*'s Chicago edition two days a week, not exactly mass penetration for Chicago. Its editor, James O'Shea, hopes to raise $8–10 million to keep the effort going and admirably refuses a salary (in contrast to ProPublica's director, who makes $570,000 a year, and the analogous Texas *Tribune* foundation-funded Web site, which pays its editor $315,000—salaries that show that pro-bono journalism has not yet shed all capitalist values).

Salaries aside, the Texas *Tribune* seeks to "build a durable model for journalism in the future."[15] The site's chief funder sees it as permanent watchdog on the local scene, making up for all the cuts in the traditional papers. Some of its reporters feel that working for a Web site, even one in an experimental stage, is safer than staying on at the old papers, with their endless cutbacks. This may well be as important a shift as any. The owners of the press have been so ruthless in trying to maintain their unrealistic profits that they have demoralized their chief asset: their own staffs. Even though these new projects may not all survive or reach the public they aim for, they at least offer hope, something that the newspapers increasingly lack.

There is also promise in a new analogous university involvement in this area, just as there has been in book publishing. A project called Under-Told Stories has been started by Saint John's University in Minnesota, which has researched local changes for both press and documentary treatment. The Columbia report cites several other promising examples.[16] Journalism students at Florida International University have found many local papers, including the much depleted *Miami Herald*, willing to use

---

15   David Carr, "News Erupts, and So Does a Web Debut," *New York Times*, November 9, 2009, B1.
16   Downie, Jr. and Schudson, 59.

their reporting. The University of California at Berkeley and Columbia both have Web sites for the stories dug up by its journalism students, as do schools in Maryland, Boston, and Phoenix. The University of Missouri has run its own daily newspaper since its journalism school opened in 1908, even though the paper regularly loses money. As local coverage shrinks along with diminishing budgets, this may well be a useful step, though with the same caveats against institutionalizing the weaknesses of the existing media.

But as helpful as the work of these students is, it cannot effectively substitute for the knowledge and networks of professionals, who have covered a local or state government beat for years and know where the bodies are buried. And yet increasingly, American papers may no longer have a choice and readers will be grateful for whatever news they can get.

In Europe, by contrast, as the Columbia report reluctantly agrees, even in countries with conservative governments, major programs have been initiated to help the press financially, and vast amounts allocated to at least preserve the status quo. Berlusconi's Italy already spends over 700 million euros a year, largely in postal subsidies, underwriting the Italian press, much of which, of course, belongs to Berlusconi himself. In France, Sarkozy convened an Estates General of the Press, which came out this year with a report proposing a similar level of support. The plan addressed some of the structural weaknesses of the press, such as the prohibitively high costs of production and distribution, offered helpful reforms for coping with excessively high labor costs, and allocated much-needed cash. But the plan was not intended to propose new approaches to the questions we have been discussing. Money was not allocated for improving coverage or for dealing with the Web. The plan's primary aim was to shore up the papers just as they were. At first, the government proposed to increase potential readership by give a free year's subscription to every 18-year-old. Cooler heads prevailed and a more reasonable experiment was proposed: one free issue a week for a year of any of France's 60 dailies to the first 200,000 youngsters (now defined as 18–24) who wrote in. The response was unexpected: within the first few days, all slots were filled, and the requests were not overwhelmingly for *L'Equipe*, the daily sports paper, as many had feared they would be. (It was at the insistence of France's new cultural minister, Frederic Mitterand, that the paper was included, in a deliberate attempt to cross class lines.) Surprisingly, *Le Monde* came in first, chosen by 19 percent of the applicants. *L'Equipe* was requested by close to half that number, as were *Liberation* and *Le Figaro*. This suggests that the young may not be as opposed to print journalism as many feared and confirms the reasons for the success of the free dailies. (This idea was based on a trial by the regional daily *Ouest-France*, the paper that actually enjoys the highest circulation in France. The paper gave young readers a year's trial subscription and was very pleased when 15 percent of the recipients chose to continue it afterward at their own expense. But while such an encouraging result will doubtless help to maintain morale, it does not address the major issues of declining income facing the press in the future.

Bringing the example of the BBC into the discussion raises a fundamental question. Why is the press primarily dependent on advertising for its revenue? This was not so at the beginning. Copies of eighteenth-century newspapers do not contain any ads. Indeed, in the United States, newspapers received considerable governmental aid from the outset. Benjamin Franklin, the country's first post-master general, understood the importance of a national press in uniting the disparate and far-flung former colonies. Papers were given favorable treatment in postage rates and received indirect government subsidies. Alexis de Tocqueville, on visiting America, was struck by both the quality and quantity of local newspapers and wrote admiringly about them, though he was also struck by the fact that advertising was beginning to play an important role. In his *Democracy in America*, he wrote, "There is hardly a town in the United States without a newspaper . . . Because it is easy to start a newspaper, anybody can do it. On the other hand, the competition is such that newspapers cannot expect to earn very large profits, which discourages people with great business acumen from embarking on this kind of venture."[17] (Ironically, it is only during the recent neoconservative years that the US government has begun to argue against these postal subsidies, negative measures that have also been proposed by the neoliberals in the European Union.)

This generation and previous ones were brought up on the fallacious notion that advertising in the press, television, and now the Internet assures "free" content. It is a common cliché to ask how much the several pounds of newsprint in the Sunday edition of the *New York Times* would cost the reader if it were not for ads. But I would argue that far from assuring free content, ads merely function as a private tax that customers pay indirectly. Advertising expenses are figured along with production costs in determining the price of the product advertised.

---

17   Alexis de Tocqueville, *Democracy in America*, New York: Library of America, 2004, 210–1.

When, over the years, I have calculated the price of any given book, I have always figured in the 10 percent allocated to ads, just as I included the author's royalty. We all pay for the ads whenever we purchase anything, indirectly covering the cost of the persuasion designed to sell these objects to us.

The advertising industry has tried to persuade us that ads, by reaching a vast audience, turned products into mass-market items, which made them cheaper. But anyone looking carefully at the pricing of products knows that this is not the case. Prices are usually the highest that the manufacturer feels the market will bear—usually the same price charged by his competitors. We have only to notice how the prices of different brands rise together, each manufacturer wishing to assure his firm the same profit. Indeed, the disproof of the advertisers' argument can be seen in any supermarket. The only really cheap items are generic, or house brands bearing the label of the store that sells it, and these are cheaper precisely because they are *not* advertised.

In addition, advertisers' pressure on media to reach the widest possible number of customers has been responsible for a continuous and systematic lowering of content. We forget the importance of the intellectual content that used to exist in TV and radio. In France, under De Gaulle, TV viewers could still see performances of Sartre's plays. In the UK, the BBC was able to publish one of the country's most interesting weeklies, *The Listener*, which was based on that week's broadcasts. As Pierre Bourdieu[18] and others have written, much intellectual discourse has disappeared from the mass media precisely because of the pressure to maximize audiences for the sake of the advertisers, though

---

18   Pierre Bourdieu, *On Television*, New York: The New Press, 1999.

there are exceptions in the governmentally subsidized media created specifically to counter these trends, such as the radio programs of France Culture or NPR or to a lesser extent the Franco-German public television network Arte.

This is not to argue that the BBC has totally escaped such pressure, above all since the creation of other networks meant specifically to compete with it for the same audience. In recent years, it has faced increasing criticism for becoming more like its commercial rivals, raising its salaries to match theirs and lowering its content accordingly. But the original charter of the BBC, which stated that the network's role was to educate and to entertain, was not based on audience surveys. The network was an independent, nongovernmental entity, managed by a board of twelve people charged with protecting the quality of the broadcasts and serving the public interest. The BBC, first in radio then in TV, was meant to broadcast what it felt was best for its audiences. To that end, a tax—or license fee—was placed first on all radios and then on television sets. The government had the police powers to locate and fine any unlicensed receivers, and its monitoring trucks still ply British streets.

The BBC model was widely imitated, first throughout the British Commonwealth and then in Europe. As we have seen, the Norwegians deliberately copied the British example, and I pay a license fee annually to the French government for my television set, even though I find the BBC's news programs of far higher quality than their French counterparts (though the overseas broadcasts of the BBC are partly paid for by their Foreign Office, just as are the news broadcasts of France 24).

The logical or perhaps literal US equivalent of this would be to place a tax on all computers to help pay for the news content they now distribute free. That would be close to the French charge on photocopying machines: users must pay a fee for every page copied from a published book not in the public domain. But such a tax would be difficult to control and impossible to impose on the hundreds of millions, if not billions, of users in developing countries. Nor, I would argue, would it be morally right to limit their access to the information that the West has been able to produce.

But there is another, and simpler, way of establishing a fee. As we have seen, Google and other access providers constantly use the content of newspapers to attract and interest their users. This, in turn, allows them to charge more and more for their ads and increase their phenomenal profits. According to the *New York Times*, Google had very close to 50 billion queries in July 2008 alone, the equivalent of 65 million hits every hour. It absorbed 25 percent of all Internet ads in the US in 2006 and an estimated 30 percent in 2007.[19] In 2004, its profits were $3 billion; at the start of 2008, these had gone up to $4.85 billion for an annual turnover of $19.6 billion, a rate practically high enough to please the Baron de Seillière. In 2008, the value of the firm was placed at $200 billion—more than enough to endow the *New York Times* and many other papers.

I am not arguing here for the public ownership of Google, though that would be an interesting case to make. I am simply suggesting that either its profits or its ad revenue be taxed to help the press gather the very news that features so prominently on its Web pages and attracts so many of its readers. TV ads are already taxed in France to support the film industry. It makes excellent sense to tax the ads on the

19   Poulet, 47.

Internet or else the resulting profits. The people at Google have neither contributed to the invention of the Net nor helped gather the news that they use so successfully. There is no reason why they, and other access providers, should not pay for it. These taxes might be easier to implement than some of those proposed by McChesney and Nichols, though a real public debate might clarify which solutions are the most feasible.

Whether that news would in future be disseminated on the Web or on the printed page or on both is an important debate but it is ultimately of secondary interest. What matters is that newspapers be able to continue in their traditional role of news gathering and analysis and perhaps even improve on what they have been able to do in previous decades. The crucial question is how to pay to insure that they will continue to do so.

I don't agree with David Swensen's suggestion that all of $5 billion would be required to endow the *New York Times* or any other paper. The *Times* will continue to have other sources of income and will not need to live entirely off the interest of an endowment. When we started the New Press as an independent not-for-profit publishing house in 1990, we did so with about $1 million of foundation help. This allowed us to begin publishing a list that now totals a thousand titles, with some eighty new books added each year and with sales of close to $6 million. Though we still need help to cover those areas where a loss is assured, we would not have needed a huge endowment to pay for these losses (nice as such an endowment might have been).

Likewise, the *Times* and others can define the difference between their earned income and the amounts needed to supplement that. Nor does it need to continue to pay its extremely high salaries and treat its staff to regal expenses.

I remember years ago visiting the official apartment of the *Times* correspondent in London, which would have been perfectly suitable for an ambassador. Clearly, the *Times* felt its correspondent was only barely less important a representative of the United States. The lodgings were indeed so officially stuffy that its then relatively young inhabitants felt understandably uncomfortable there. The *Times*'s overall salaries are now so high that many feel they alienate its journalists from the cares and concerns of ordinary folk. The purpose here is not to rewrite the *Times*'s budget but simply to state that Swensen's figures, based on the status quo, may not be what is really needed for the *Times*—and other papers—to fulfill their proper function. This has in effect been proved by the *Times*'s ability to cut half a billion dollars from last year's expenses, even if not all of those cuts were ones you might have chosen. What we need to understand fully is the nature and scope of the press's deficits and the amount of tax income that would be needed to replace it. As with the BBC's funding, this money should be funneled through an independent entity, charged with making sure that the press is kept free and clear of political influence. The amounts clearly would differ from country to country and might be supplemented by taxes on the search engines and their forms of advertising, as I have suggested above.

These taxes, I understand, would ultimately be passed on to the consumer, as they are now. So is the increasing amount of governmental aid now being given to the press in Europe. But they should provide a sound and permanent financial base for the press that would be sufficiently indirect that it would not raise public opposition much more than existing media license fees do now. The public has accepted these as the price for the BBC and other television networks throughout Europe. On the whole, the system has worked straightforwardly and assured the necessary income, though obviously criticisms can be made. It is, however, a simple and effective precedent. I would argue that such a solution might well gain the support of ordinary readers as well as of journalists themselves. It seems time for such approaches to be investigated further and debated not only in the press but also in legislatures throughout the world.

Conclusion: Technology and Monopoly

As we have seen, the world of words is in full transition. The old structures of ownership have either been transformed into large globalized conglomerates—as in publishing—or greatly weakened, as in the world of newspapers in the United States and much of Europe. The old assumption that private capital will continue to invest in traditional media—books, newspapers, and quality cinema and broadcasting—has been undermined by the perception that returns for such investments are inadequate, compared with the huge profits that bankers and stock market traders have been able to make through speculation and gambling in other areas.

This book has examined some of the ways in which new forms of support for traditional media can be created. Governmental aid at all levels can ensure the survival of many such enterprises, from small independent bookstores to major newspapers. New structures are needed to allow for the creation of cooperative entities or not-for-profits—which have become the focus of much of the debate in the United States, though not yet in France. Curiously, the French government has been far more willing to offer vast new subsidies to the press, either directly or through their program of offering free copies to young people.

The challenges posed by changes in ownership and profit margins have been compounded by the technological innovations that are now sweeping the world. Newspapers have been greatly damaged by the availability of news, much of it their own, on the Internet. Book publishers and bookstores are also facing the possibility that books will become available on the Internet or through new distribution channels such as reading machines like the Kindle, the iPad, and even cell phones.

Though it is still far too early to evaluate the full impact of these new technologies, it is possible to ask some preliminary questions and consider some of the obvious dangers. Let us start with the availability of books in forms other than the traditional printed page. First, it is important to remember that every technological change in communications has been seen as a possible death sentence to the book. First radio and then television were viewed with alarm. American newspapers in the 1930s refused to list radio programs in their pages, so afraid were they of radio's luring away readers. Though people did indeed spend vast amounts of time listening to the radio, this did not do the major harm to books, magazines, and newspapers that many had feared. It has only been with the spread of the Internet that we have begun to see a real change in reading patterns, although, as we saw in the chapter on newspapers, only 3 percent of Americans now read their newspapers on the Internet, and that for only a few minutes a day.

The availability of books on the Internet is still relatively new and it is too early to determine the permanent effect either on sales of actual books or on reading patterns. The French publishing house La Découverte conducted an interesting experiment recently. It launched a new series of books on current issues called Zone and made all of the books available online, gratis. Half of the readers of the books took advantage of the free material on the Web, but the other half actually bought the published edition, possibly as many as might have bought the books without the experiment. The publishers are unable to determine whether some of those who began reading the books on the Web decided ultimately to buy them, that is, to what extent the books' online presence acted as free publicity on those who finally purchased copies. In any case, the series' appearance on the Web did not seem to substantially damage the books' sales or their appeal to a potential audience.

Similarly, the recent craze among Japanese teenagers for reading novels addressed to them, chapter by chapter, on their cell phones has resulted in a vast electronic reading audience, but again, not one reluctant to buy the final version in paper form.

American university presses carried out another successful experiment. Discovering that sales of monographs had fallen to an average of 350 copies—that was the number of university libraries throughout the world that wanted a complete selection of scholarly output—the university presses decided to publish a number of such titles on the Web. Following a persuasive argument by Robert Darnton, the American historian of reading, the Mellon Foundation agreed to pay the considerable cost of editing the manuscripts. Once on the Web, the monographs could be downloaded free of charge, though having the pages printed out and bound would cost a reader a good part of what the published book might have. But because the audience was so small and clearly defined, the experiment made sense. By contrast, the tens of thousands of writers who have placed their manuscripts on the Web in the hope of reaching an audience beyond their immediate family have been disappointed. Clearly, the Web works when there is a defined audience that has a specific need for a book, but an unknown author has less of a chance of reaching a new reader than do the millions of unknown bloggers.

In addition to these experiments, there was a widely hailed attempt at placing printing facilities in bookstores, but this failed completely. Those betting on this enterprise argued that stores would no longer need to stock old titles and that customers could simply order a copy of whatever they needed. But publishers can now use print-on-demand technology to make small quantities available in the traditional way, so the need for printing machines in the bookstores was obviated.

It is doubtful that the new reading machines will meet such a fate. It is too early to see how widespread these machines will become or whether their prices will decline substantially as the market for them grows (I still remember being given one of the very first ballpoint pens—which cost an enormous $20 at the time). Whatever the eventual cost of the machines and whatever their success, it is clear now that they represent a major threat to writers and publishers. Even though only 3 to 5 percent of new books now appear on these machines, that proportion is bound to increase. Wanting to achieve a nearly monopolistic control of this new distribution system, Amazon, Google, and now book chains such as Barnes & Noble have set out to control all the financial factors involved. Amazon, having decided that the price of downloading a new book should be $9.99, whatever its length, has tried to dictate to writers and publishers exactly what their royalties or share of the price should be. Obviously, the authors and their publishers are the ones who have done all the work in creating the books and making them available, yet they are being offered a fraction of what they would get if the books were sold in the traditional way. (An American author can count on a royalty of 15 percent from a book after 10,000 copies, which comes to $4.00 or more on most books, as opposed to a putative $2.00 on an Amazon edition.) Publishers likewise would receive a smaller profit. The *New York Times* on February 28, 2010, calculated that on a $26 book—the average hardcover price—publishers earn roughly $4 of profit before overhead, but on a $9.99 e-book their profit might be as low as $3.50. On a $13 e-book, the publishers' profit would range between $4.56 and $5.54.[1] But that only takes into account initial profits. Normally, much of the money made on a book comes from its paperback edition. Those editions would, in all likelihood, disappear, since paperback prices are now in the range of e-book prices— $9 to $10 for a mass-market paperback and $13–15 for the more common trade paperback editions. Beyond that, by relying increasingly on e-books, the publishers would be helping to destroy their major distribution network, the bookstores. Amazon et al. can count on making their profits by selling the machinery, and meanwhile the publishers are caught in a trap that makes them increasingly unable to compete with the e-book manufacturers.

The major French publishers have been meeting to decide on an alternative to the Amazon plan, but even they would be caught up in the problem of destroying their far stronger network of bookstores. Amazon's mail-order

---

1   Motoko Rich, "Math of Publishing Meets the E-Book," *New York Times*, February 28, 2010, B1.

enterprise is already a major challenge, and this new technology could be even more of a threat to the already struggling bookstores.

As this book was being completed, a new battle had broken out between Amazon and several major American publishers. Rebelling against Amazon's insistence on the under-$10 price, the Macmillan group insisted on the higher price of $15 for all of their titles sought by Amazon. Macmillan is owned by the German Holzbrink corporation and includes a number of important American houses, such as Farrar, Straus and Giroux. Amazon's immediate reaction was to remove all Macmillan titles from its Web site. Since Amazon controls from 15 to 20 percent of all retail book sales, this was an effective negotiating stance, though one that I would have thought would bring antitrust accusations, if not actual government lawsuits, against Amazon. Perhaps Amazon was aware of that danger, for they eventually pulled back and agreed to the higher price.[2] They thus fell into line with the higher price range that Apple had conceded to five of the country's largest publishers, Hachette, HarperCollins, and Penguin, all foreign-owned, and Simon & Schuster and Macmillan itself. The *Times* assumed that Amazon was willing to limit profits on e-books initially in order to sell more of its Kindles. This follows Amazon's willingness in its early years to lose millions on its book sales in order to establish its name (and raise the price of its stock, then largely controlled by its owner).

In the meantime, Google is now digitizing millions of public domain books, on which it will pay no royalties at all but will in time be able to charge readers whatever

2   Motoko Rich and Brad Stone, "Publisher Wins Fight with Amazon Over E-books," *New York Times*, February 1, 2010, B1.

the market bears. Nor is there any guarantee as to what other conditions it may impose. In a recent discussion at the Centre Pompidou with the chief librarian of Lyons, I asked about these possibilities. Lyons, which boasts France's second-greatest library, had been refused funds by the government to digitize its collections. It was a typical Sarkozy move, and it forced the library to turn to Google, in effect privatizing its holdings. (This situation has become very common in American universities, which have increasingly had to raise the money for scientific research by effectually selling the results from their labs to private companies.) I asked whether any conditions had been imposed on Google's exploitation of the library. Could Google, for instance, decide to place an ad for Coca-Cola on every page or use the names of the readers for their own advertising campaigns? Even these extreme examples failed to elicit a negative answer. The library had imposed no conditions on its bargain with Google.

Happily, European publishers and governments have begun to explore alternatives to joining Google's and Amazon's would-be international monopolies. But these two firms are way ahead of any potential rivals and thus far very little has been done to control their monopolistic policies. Like Google's massive, unpaid use of the news, Google and Amazon's potential mass takeover of library holdings is a major threat.

Professor Darnton, who recently agreed to take on the direction of Harvard's libraries, has written a series of persuasive articles in the *New York Review of Books* on the dangers inherent in the Google plan. In the most recent of these, he looks at the different lawsuits that are winding

their way through the courts.[3] Google had worked
out a preliminary agreement with groups representing
American authors and publishers, which was basically that
it would pay a small royalty on copyrighted books, and in
turn charge a "moderate" fee to universities and libraries for access to the ten million books it has already digitized plus the books still to be digitized—potentially more
than 20 million. But what this fees will be is not defined
exactly, and in fact by giving Google what will in effect be
a monopoly, the agreement grants the company the power
to charge whatever it wishes. Remembering the very high
profit it already makes, close to 25 percent on its $22 billion
of annual income, one cannot be overly optimistic about
its future restraint. The agreement has been the subject of
a number of lawsuits charging that it violates American
antitrust legislation, and over 400 memoranda have been
filed in the matter.[4] The case is now before a New York
judge and may have been decided by the time this book is
published.

The French and German governments have sent
memoranda urging the court to reject the agreement "in
its entirety," at least in so far as the citizens of their own
countries are concerned. They object to an agreement that
would give Google "unchecked, concentrated power . . .
based on a 'commercially driven' agreement negotiated 'in
secrecy.' " The French and German briefs invoke Pascal,
Descartes, Goethe, and Schiller as well as the Declaration
of the Rights of Man to defend "free access to information"
threatened by Google's "de facto monopoly."[5] (It seems a

---

3   Robert Darnton, "Google and the New Digital Future," *New York
Review of Books*, December 17, 2009.
4   Ibid., 82.
5   Ibid.

bit pathetic to me that the best these governments can do is invoke their glorious past, rather than summon the power to threaten effective anti-monopoly legislation, though to be fair they did ask the European Commission to defend their publics' interest.)

However, the European briefs in the New York case became dramatically moot when, on December 19, 2009, a lawsuit against Google brought by a number of French publishers and authors in 2006 was finally decided by a Paris court. The court declared that "Google infringed copyrights by digitizing books and putting extracts online without the authorizations" of the books' publishers and authors. The court ordered Google to pay a substantial 300,000 euros in damages and to stop their French digitization program. An additional fine of 10,000 euros a day would be due until Google removed the French material from its database.[6]

At the same time, the Sarkozy government reversed its previous position and decided that it, not Google, would scan French literature, historic documents, and its own audiovisual archives. Sarkozy announced that 750 million euros would be allocated for this. In effect, he implemented the program that Darnton had hoped would be possible in the US (more on that below).

The German press has also stepped in with a major antitrust complaint.[7] German newspapers and magazines want Google to pay for the excerpts it runs from their pages. Google responded with its usual argument that it was actually helping the papers. The journals answered

---

6 Matthew Saltmarsh, "Google Loses in French Copyright Case," *New York Times*, December 19, 2009, B3.
7 Eric Pfanner, "An Antitrust Complaint for Google in Germany," *New York Times*, January 19, 2010, B4.

that all the German press Web sites together made only 100 million euros in ads, while Google made 1.2 billion euros in Germany alone. Thus far, the German Federal Cartel Office has not said how they plan to respond. Similar complaints have been voiced by newspapers in Belgium and Italy. None wants to pull its Web site out of the Google system, but they all hope for some form of compensation.

Whether any of this will have an effect on the US lawsuit has yet to be seen. But given the prevailing opposition to using foreign precedents, we can assume that the American suit will proceed as if all of this had never happened. Though the American Department of Justice has also been involved in the New York case, it has admitted from the start that it did not want "the opportunity or momentum to be lost." Its objections have been relatively technical and limited, saying nothing about controlling prices, protecting privacy or avoiding censorship. Google's basic agreement amazingly allows it to exclude up to 15 percent of works it has digitized from its accessible database![8]

Darnton goes on to outline what he feels would be the best solution to the problem, though it is not one currently being discussed and would require new legislation, rather than a court decision. Basically, he argues for turning the Google database into a public one, a resource that would be available to everyone free of charge, just like our network of libraries. This comes close to the possibility I invoked above, of public ownership of Google, or at least of a part of its activities. It is a persuasive case, similar to the public ownership of the airwaves, which every country has asserted. In many ways, the Internet, developed with public money and intended to be free, fits logically

---

8   Darnton, 84.

into such a framework. Especially since in this case we are talking about access to a common cultural heritage that is already available from libraries throughout the world....

Darnton admits that such a solution is unlikely to be legislated in the United States today and argues for a fall-back position of having a free public digitization of all the books in the Library of Congress and, presumably, its equivalents in other countries. But even if the US Congress is unlikely to take such bold steps, there is no reason why the European Union might not consider his ideas. Google's powers are not yet unlimited, and the threat of legislation limiting its power and its profits might even persuade it to cooperate with such public schemes.

In citing the arguments against Google's monopoly I do not mean to imply that the availability of all these books on the Internet is not of great value, provided they are free and not part of someone's hidden agenda of profit, advertising, and the building of valuable mailing lists. Indeed, we should ask what use might be made of a free and public Web. Should new books not be made available after a number of years, free of charge? After all, many books are republished in less expensive paperback editions after a year or so. Should we consider the possibility of a book being posted and accessible without charge after five or ten years? The author could be paid for this by the state, in the way that authors now are in several European countries for copies made available through public libraries.

The argument is even stronger for technical and scientific books, which are far too expensive to be bought in developing countries. An impressive start was made recently by MIT, which, with foundation funding, placed its entire curriculum on the Web for free use by the public. (Compare this with the stance adopted by Columbia

University and other schools that claimed they owned every word a professor uttered and could charge for these on the Web.) A revolution in instruction might be possible in the poorer countries if these curricula and the books they entail were to be made available gratis, supported if need be by the foreign aid budgets of the richer countries.

Ironically, the Web's huge potential in this respect has been increasingly limited by ever more draconian copyright restrictions. Copyright protections keep on being extended, thanks partly to expensive corporate lobbying. The last American extension, known to many as the Mickey Mouse Protection Act, came in 2003 when Disney realized that some of its most valuable properties would soon be in the public domain. They successfully lobbied the US Congress to extend copyright by another twenty years, bringing the total period to nearly a hundred years, twice the length of time provided by the copyright act originally. Disney, many of whose productions have been based on the free use (or plagiarizing) of the world's classics (How much would Victor Hugo have been paid for *The Hunchback of Notre Dame?*), was assured of 20 additional years of copyright, as were some 400,000 other works, including many basic products of American culture of the 1920s, from Robert Frost to George Gershwin, though these were accidental contemporaries of Mickey Mouse and not necessarily works that their creators would have wanted to see excluded from the public domain.[9]

Happily, many living authors have joined the Creative Commons movement, through which they give users free access to their work on the Web. This has had some effect

---

9   David Boller, *Viral Spiral*, New York: The New Press, 2008, 73.

in counteracting the repeated extensions of the copyright act. But corporate lobbying in the Congress has unfortunately been far more effective than these laudable efforts to counterbalance it.

The battles over copyright extension are just part of the war being waged over control of the Web. The major American companies are also spending fortunes lobbying in Washington for technical changes that would give them important advantages over their rivals.[10] Again, this shows the power of political decisions, even those taken behind the scenes, in determining the future of what is clearly the most important medium of communication in the coming decades.

Unfortunately, the questions involved are often too esoteric to attract enough attention, and the press has been delinquent, in every country, in not covering issues that will determine much of our common future. It is time for the political parties to recognize that the debate on the division of media spoils is as important as past debates over other national resources, and needs public examination and discussion. It is understandable that in a period of severe economic crisis, these issues of access to the media seem marginal and esoteric. But it is important to remember that independent media, whether books or newspapers, are essential to any real debate of precisely the issues that underlie this crisis and its possible solution.

As we have seen, there are still many areas in which individual decisions are crucial. Everyone has the power to choose to support a newspaper or independent bookseller. Authors can decide to move their work to small,

---

10   For more details on this subject, see *Digital Democracy* by Jeff Chester, New York: The New Press, 2007.

independent houses, and those who run these at great personal sacrifice can decide to continue and even extend their efforts.

But the context in which these private decisions are made depends on political decisions. Governments can choose to help support their cultural infrastructure, as the Norwegian government has done. Regional entities, and towns and villages, can do the same, even when their national governments have followed the new neoliberal policy of allowing every decision to be controlled by profit. But some major decisions, such as the future of Google, have to be taken at a national and even international level. It is here that political debate and commitment become essential.

The world of words and money is but a microcosm of the larger world whose changes have transformed our countries and our cultures. But these changes that have had such an effect on all our lives are not necessarily permanent. Other paths are open. It is for us to choose to follow them.

Index